24.60

The Arab-Israeli Conflict

Shasta Gaughen, *Book Editor*

Daniel Leone, *President*
Bonnie Szumski, *Publisher*
Scott Barbour, *Managing Editor*
Brenda Stalcup, *Series Editor*

Contemporary Issues
Companion

GREENHAVEN
PRESS®

THOMSON
——————
GALE

San Diego • Detroit • New York • San Francisco • Cleveland
New Haven, Conn. • Waterville, Maine • London • Munich

For more information, contact
Greenhaven Press
27500 Drake Rd.
Farmington Hills, MI 48331-3535
Or you can visit our Internet site at http://www.gale.com

LIBRARY OF CONGRESS CATALOGING-IN-PUBLICATION DATA

The Arab-Israeli conflict / Shasta Gaughen, book editor.
    p. cm. — (Contemporary issues companion)
Includes bibliographical references and index.
ISBN 0-7377-1616-9 (pbk. : alk. paper) — ISBN 0-7377-1615-0 (lib. : alk. paper)
    1. Arab-Israeli conflict—1993– —Peace. 2. Al-Aqsa Intifada, 2000– 3. Israel—
Politics and government—1993– 4. Palestinian Arabs—Politics and
government—1993– I. Gaughen, Shasta. II. Series.
DS119.76.A725 2004
956.9405'4—dc21   2003049059

Contents

Foreword   5

Introduction   7

Chapter 1: The History of the Arab-Israeli Conflict

1. The Middle East Before the Creation of Modern Israel   13
   David Schafer

2. One Land, Two People: The Birth of Modern Israel   21
   J.J. Goldberg and Phil Sudo

3. The Troubled History of the Occupied Territories   25
   Ruth Margolies Beitler

4. The Oslo Accords and the Demise of the Peace Process   33
   Baylis Thomas

5. Shattered Hopes for Peace in the New Century   43
   Peter Vilbig

Chapter 2: Arab and Israeli Approaches to the Conflict

1. The Cycle of Violence: An Overview   49
   Serge Schmemann

2. Terror Tactics Are Official Palestinian Policy   53
   Martin Peretz

3. Palestinians Resort to Terror Tactics Out of Despair   58
   Eyad El Sarraj, interviewed by Linda Butler

4. Israel's Response to Palestinian Terrorism Is Justified   65
   Facts and Logic About the Middle East

5. Israel's Military Actions Against Palestinians Are Unwarranted   68
   Edward W. Said

6. Religious Extremism: A Problem on Both Sides   73
   Allan C. Brownfeld

Chapter 3: Living with the Arab-Israeli Conflict

1. Five Days in the Middle East   80
   Time

2. Families on Both Sides Struggle with Loss   89
   Thomas Fields-Meyer

3. When the War Hits Home: Mothers' Stories   94
   Matt Rees

4. A Day in the Life of an Israeli Woman   99
   Deborah French Greniman

5. A Palestinian Refugee Visits His Home   106
   John Donnelly

Chapter 4: Proposals for Creating Peace Between Israel and Palestine

1. Overcoming the Obstacles to Peace   114
   Cherie R. Brown
2. Israel Must Abandon Its Claim of Being a Jewish Homeland   119
   Allan C. Brownfeld
3. Giving Up Land Will Not Create Peace   125
   Colin Leci
4. The United States Should Implement a Settlement   130
   Sherwin Wine
5. What We Can Do   136
   Henry A. Kissinger

Glossary   141

Chronology   143

Organizations to Contact   150

Bibliography   153

Index   155

FOREWORD

In the news, on the streets, and in neighborhoods, individuals are confronted with a variety of social problems. Such problems may affect people directly: A young woman may struggle with depression, suspect a friend of having bulimia, or watch a loved one battle cancer. And even the issues that do not directly affect her private life—such as religious cults, domestic violence, or legalized gambling—still impact the larger society in which she lives. Discovering and analyzing the complexities of issues that encompass communal and societal realms as well as the world of personal experience is a valuable educational goal in the modern world.

Effectively addressing social problems requires familiarity with a constantly changing stream of data. Becoming well informed about today's controversies is an intricate process that often involves reading myriad primary and secondary sources, analyzing political debates, weighing various experts' opinions—even listening to firsthand accounts of those directly affected by the issue. For students and general observers, this can be a daunting task because of the sheer volume of information available in books, periodicals, on the evening news, and on the Internet. Researching the consequences of legalized gambling, for example, might entail sifting through congressional testimony on gambling's societal effects, examining private studies on Indian gaming, perusing numerous websites devoted to Internet betting, and reading essays written by lottery winners as well as interviews with recovering compulsive gamblers. Obtaining valuable information can be time-consuming—since it often requires researchers to pore over numerous documents and commentaries before discovering a source relevant to their particular investigation.

Greenhaven's Contemporary Issues Companion series seeks to assist this process of research by providing readers with useful and pertinent information about today's complex issues. Each volume in this anthology series focuses on a topic of current interest, presenting informative and thought-provoking selections written from a wide variety of viewpoints. The readings selected by the editors include such diverse sources as personal accounts and case studies, pertinent factual and statistical articles, and relevant commentaries and overviews. This diversity of sources and views, found in every Contemporary Issues Companion, offers readers a broad perspective in one convenient volume.

In addition, each title in the Contemporary Issues Companion series is designed especially for young adults. The selections included in every volume are chosen for their accessibility and are expertly edited in consideration of both the reading and comprehension levels of the audience. The structure of the anthologies also enhances accessibility. An introductory essay places each issue in context and provides helpful facts such as historical background or current statistics and legislation that pertain to the topic. The chapters that follow organize the material and focus on specific aspects of the book's topic. Every essay is introduced by a brief summary of its main points and biographical information about the author. These summaries aid in comprehension and can also serve to direct readers to material of immediate interest and need. Finally, a comprehensive index allows readers to efficiently scan and locate content.

The Contemporary Issues Companion series is an ideal launching point for research on a particular topic. Each anthology in the series is composed of readings taken from an extensive gamut of resources, including periodicals, newspapers, books, government documents, the publications of private and public organizations, and Internet websites. In these volumes, readers will find factual support suitable for use in reports, debates, speeches, and research papers. The anthologies also facilitate further research, featuring a book and periodical bibliography and a list of organizations to contact for additional information.

A perfect resource for both students and the general reader, Greenhaven's Contemporary Issues Companion series is sure to be a valued source of current, readable information on social problems that interest young adults. It is the editors' hope that readers will find the Contemporary Issues Companion series useful as a starting point to formulate their own opinions about and answers to the complex issues of the present day.

INTRODUCTION

On May 14, 1948, David Ben-Gurion officially announced the Israeli Declaration of Independence, establishing the nation of Israel in territory that until then had been part of the British-controlled region of Palestine. Ben-Gurion, who would become the first prime minister of the new state, proclaimed that "the land of Israel was the birthplace of the Jewish people. Here their spiritual, religious and national identity was formed. Here they achieved independence and created a culture of national and universal significance. Here they wrote and gave the Bible to the world." The Jewish people's historic association with the land of Palestine gave all Jews from around the world the right to return and revive Israel as their national homeland, he maintained. Further, Ben-Gurion declared, the right of the Jewish people to form the state of Israel was supported by the United Nations.

In fact, UN Security Council Resolution 181, adopted on November 29, 1947, had explicitly mandated the partition of Palestine into separate Jewish and Arab states, with the city of Jerusalem to be administered internationally. However, while the Jews had accepted the UN partition plan, the Arabs had rejected it. Sporadic violence had already occurred as a result of this disagreement. But when Ben-Gurion declared Israel's independence, it sparked an all-out war. The day after the declaration, the fledgling state was attacked by a coalition of five Arab nations. By the end of 1948, the Israelis had gained the upper hand in the war, occupying far more territory than had been allotted to Israel under the original UN partition plan. More than half a million Arab Palestinians lost their homes; some fled the fighting, while others were forcibly driven out by Israeli soldiers.

In 1949, the United Nations implemented an armistice proposal that was intended to end the hostilities and secure a lasting peace between Israel and the neighboring Arab states. This plan included establishing permanent borders for the new nation of Israel. However, Israel's Arab neighbors refused to officially recognize the new country. Ever since the Israeli War of Independence—referred to as the *Nakba*, or disaster, by Palestinians—Israel has been continually plagued by violence and conflict. Peace between Israelis and Palestinians remains an elusive goal to this day.

Why has peace between Arabs and Israelis been so difficult to achieve? According to many observers, the Arab-Israeli conflict revolves around several key controversies, including the validity of the Jewish claim of a historic right to a homeland in the region, the Israeli occupation of Palestinian land, the establishment of Jewish settlements in the occupied territories, the Palestinian demand for an independent state, the predicament of the Palestinian refugees, acts of terrorism by Palestinians against Israelis, Israeli violence toward and repression of Palestinians, the upholding of Israel's national security, tensions over water rights, and the debate over the administration of the city of Jerusalem, which is holy to Jews and Muslims alike. While all of these divisive issues contribute to continued unrest, the refugee question, Israeli occupation and settlement, Palestinian terrorism, and Israeli repression are among the most difficult to resolve.

The refugee issue has been at the heart of peace negotiations since the end of the 1948 war. On December 11, 1948, the UN General Assembly passed Resolution 194, declaring that "refugees wishing to return to their homes and live at peace with their neighbors should be permitted to do so at the earliest practicable date." Nevertheless, the Israeli government did not allow many Palestinian refugees to return. Instead, the Palestinian refugee problem was exacerbated in 1967 with the onset of the Six-Day War between Israel and the coalition of Egypt, Jordan, and Syria. In spite of the fact that the combined Arab forces were far superior to those of the Israeli military, by the end of the war Israel had scored a decisive victory, dramatically expanding its borders by annexing the West Bank, the Gaza Strip, the Sinai Desert, and the Golan Heights. The war created hundreds of thousands of new refugees and introduced a new controversy into the peace process: the continuous occupation of Palestinian territories by Israel.

According to the MidEast Web for Coexistence, there are currently 4.6 million Palestinian refugees, 3.9 million of whom are registered with the United Nations Relief and Works Agency for Palestinian Refugees (UNRWA). Over a million refugees live in camps administered by the UNRWA, often in conditions of dire poverty and overcrowding. Many of the Palestinian refugees—both those who were born in Palestine and those who were born in the camps—still want to return to the land and houses that their families used to own, regardless of the number of years or decades that have passed. The United Nations has continued to support the Palestinian refugees' desire to return to their original homes; in 1967, it reinforced Resolution 194 by the passage of UN Security Council Resolution 242, which called for a fair solution to the problem. Palestinians believe that these UN resolutions embody their "right of return," making it illegal for Israel to keep them from reclaiming their ancestral lands and properties.

But this situation is complicated by the fact that over the years, the land that used to belong to Palestinian refugees has been occupied by Israelis. The Israeli government does not relish the prospect of evicting Jewish families from homes they have lived in for as long as thirty, forty, or fifty years. Another Israeli objection to accepting the return of millions of Palestinian refugees is that Arabs would then outnumber Jews in Israel. Many Israelis fear that such an outcome would spell the end to Israel's self-determination and its existence as a

Israel and Occupied Territories

Jewish state—which, they argue, is exactly what surrounding Arab nations want to see happen.

Another facet of this problem is Israel's occupation of the Palestinian territories of the West Bank and the Gaza Strip. The 1993 Oslo Peace Accords outlined a plan in which Israel would withdraw from the occupied territories in exchange for peace. However, the peace process stalled in 1996; in the meantime, the founding of Jewish settlements in the occupied territories has continued apace. Even if Israel were to return the West Bank and Gaza to Palestinian rule, more than half a million Israeli Jews now live in these areas. As reported in the Canadian newsmagazine *Maclean's* in 1998, for example, Jews who have established settlements in Hebron—which is located in the West

Bank, outside Israel's official borders—contend that they have a right to reinstate a Jewish presence in places that are sacred to Jewish faith and history. Arabs, on the other hand, maintain that the Israeli government is allowing continued Jewish settlement in order to undermine the viability of a potential Palestinian state.

The Palestinian reaction to Israeli policies, including those regarding refugees and occupation, has frequently led to violent conflict in the streets of Israel. Those who sympathize with the Palestinian cause often argue that Palestinian terrorist acts stem from the built-up frustrations of more than fifty years of subjugation by Israel and the seemingly endless struggle to reclaim their historic homeland. These commentators insist that the continuation of the Israeli occupation of Palestinian territories, a string of right-wing Israeli prime ministers, and the ineffectiveness of Palestinian leader Yasser Arafat in brokering an acceptable peace have all led many Palestinians to feel that violence is their only option. However, supporters of Israel typically maintain that Palestinian terrorism is the direct result of policies implemented by Arafat. They contend that Arafat encourages terrorist attacks because his ultimate goal is not simply the founding of an independent Palestine but the complete eradication of Israel. According to these critics, Israeli measures against terrorism—such as sending tanks into the occupied territories or destroying the homes of suspected terrorists—are a justifiable reaction to Palestinian violence.

Despite the complex difficulties presented by the contentious issues that fuel the Arab-Israeli conflict, the Israelis and the Palestinians have more than once come close to achieving peace. Most recently, Israelis and Palestinians appeared to be making steady progress toward a permanent peace agreement during the late 1990s. In January 1997, officials from both sides signed the Hebron agreement, in which Israel agreed to reduce its military presence in the West Bank and the Gaza Strip. In October 1998, Israeli and Arab leaders signed the Wye Memorandum (named for the Maryland conference center where the negotiations took place), which gave Palestinians more authority in the West Bank in exchange for an increased effort to stop terrorist attacks against Israel. Even more tellingly, in December 1998, the Palestinian National Council revoked the clauses in its charter that explicitly called for the destruction of Israel. By the summer of 2000, concessions by both sides seemed to indicate that a lasting peace was imminent. During August 2000, Arafat and the Israeli prime minister, Ehud Barak, met with U.S. president Bill Clinton at Camp David, Maryland, in order to negotiate a new peace settlement. However, the negotiations failed, and no peace agreement was reached.

On September 28, 2000, shortly after the failed Camp David negotiations, Ariel Sharon, a member of the Israeli Parliament, paid a visit to the al-Aqsa Mosque on the Temple Mount, a place sacred to both

Muslims and Jews. Sharon was accompanied by an armed guard that was one thousand members strong. Many Muslims perceived Sharon's visit to the mosque and the presence of the armed guard as a major insult to their faith. Enraged Palestinians embarked on a wave of violence that has become known as the al-Aqsa intifada.

In February 2001, Sharon was elected prime minister of Israel. Over the next year, Palestinian suicide attacks increased dramatically, leaving numerous Israelis dead or wounded. In response to the violence, Sharon ordered tanks into the West Bank and barricaded Arafat in his government compound for weeks. Ultimately, Sharon directed the tanks to leave and let Arafat go free. But hopes for the continuance of peace negotiations were shattered by these events and by the escalating violence in the region. It was not until May 2003 that both sides again started to make tentative steps toward a new peace agreement, the so-called "road map to peace" based on the Mitchell Report. As of this writing, however, terrorist attacks by Palestinians and retaliatory strikes by the Israeli military continue unabated. Clearly, the obstacles to peace between Israel and the Palestinians have yet to be overcome.

Achieving a lasting peace in the Middle East is one of the most vital challenges in the world today. The *Arab-Israeli Conflict: Contemporary Issues Companion* presents a wide variety of viewpoints and opinions concerning this persistent problem. Authors discuss the history of Israel and Palestine in order to give context to the current state of affairs. Subsequent chapters cover the controversial tactics employed by each side in the conflict and examine various proposals for achieving peace. Rounding out the anthology are personal accounts of what life is like for individuals on both sides of the conflict. The articles included in this timely and relevant volume provide readers with helpful insights concerning the ongoing tensions between the Arabs and the Israelis, as well as the potential for peace.

CHAPTER 1

THE HISTORY OF THE ARAB-ISRAELI CONFLICT

Contemporary Issues
Companion

THE MIDDLE EAST BEFORE THE CREATION OF MODERN ISRAEL

David Schafer

Retired physiologist David Schafer is a consulting editor for the *Humanist*, a bimonthly magazine that takes a critical approach to social issues. In the following selection, Schafer probes the origins of the current conflict between Israelis and Palestinians. He covers the early relationship between Jews, Christians, and Muslims in the region, emphasizing that at one time religious tolerance was the rule rather than the exception in the Middle East. He also describes the birth of the Zionist movement during the nineteenth century, as well as the first waves of immigration of European Jews to Palestine. In addition, the author explains, the British presence in the Middle East during the 1800s and early 1900s had a significant impact on the development of contemporary Israel. While Schafer's account ends in the 1930s, he demonstrates that all the elements of today's conflict were in place before modern Israel even existed.

When a problem gets so vast and so complex that it's hard to see how it can ever be resolved, it's perfectly natural to ask ourselves whether there was a time when, with sufficient foresight, it might have been prevented. If only we knew how to anticipate such problems, we tell ourselves, maybe we could avoid them in the future. So, applying that reasoning, let us ask how the seemingly intractable mess between the Palestinian people and the state of Israel ever got started?

Who Is to Blame?

We could blame it on Sarai, wife of Abram. According to the story in Genesis 16, it was Sarai's idea, when she was still childless in her late seventies, for Abram to have a child by her Egyptian handmaid, Hagar—so he did, and named the son Ishmael. But thirteen years later, according to Genesis 21, Sarai (now renamed Sarah) herself gave birth to a son by Abram (now Abraham), and this son was named Isaac. Sarah's actions led to rivalry between the descendants of Abraham's

David Schafer, "Origins of the Israeli/Palestinian Conflict," *Humanist*, vol. 62, July/August 2002, p. 14. Copyright © 2002 by the American Humanist Association. Reproduced by permission.

sons. According to traditions, Isaac became the progenitor of the Jews and Ishmael of the northern Arabs. Both sons were circumcised at God's command, but Hagar and her son were exiled to the southern desert. And exile is a major theme in both Hebrew and Arabic stories. Hagar is from the same Semitic root for emigrate as the Arabic *hijra*—the Hegira, Muhammad's emigration from Mecca to Medina in 622 CE [Common Era], which is considered the starting point of Islam.

Or we could blame it on Pope Urban II, who in 1095 CE instigated the first Crusade. The next spring, according to Karen Armstrong in *Jerusalem:*

> A band of German Crusaders massacred the Jewish communities of Speyer, Worms, and Mainz upon the Rhine. This had certainly not been the pope's intention, but it seemed ridiculous to these Crusaders to march thousands of miles to fight Muslims—about whom they knew next to nothing—when the people who had actually killed Christ (or so the Crusaders believed) were alive and well on their very doorsteps. These were the first full-scale pogroms in Europe.

The word pogrom means "devastation" in Russian, and there were many pogroms in nineteenth-century Russia. When Israeli prime minister Ariel Sharon addressed soldiers of the Israeli Defense Force at Jenin in April 2002, he reminded them that their struggle had begun "120 years ago." This could only have referred to the pogrom that followed the assassination of Czar Alexander II in 1881, when one of the plotters was found to be a young Jewish woman. The first *aliyah* ("going up" to Israel) of Jews began the very next year with the arrival of fourteen European immigrants at Jaffa in Palestine. This was an insignificant number compared to the mainly Sephardic (Spanish-Mediterranean) Jews already in Palestine and Syria (around 25,000 in 1800), some of whose family roots had been there for a long time. However, the first *aliyah* continued until 1903 and was followed by many more.

Or we might, if we choose, even blame the present troubles on Charles Darwin, whose promulgation of the idea of natural selection in the mid–nineteenth century was immediately picked up and twisted by "Social Darwinists" to support the notion that Aryans were inherently superior to the Semitic peoples and to justify anti-Semitic campaigns throughout Europe. It is important to remember, though, that whether such anti-Jewish discrimination took the form of pogroms or something less violent, it was carried out not by Palestinian Muslims but by European Christians. Those Jews who chose to emigrate to Palestine clearly saw it at the time as a better and safer place to be.

The Birth of Zionism

As far back as the 1860s a German Jew, Moses Hess, had advocated the formation of a Jewish "national home" in Palestine. At that time most

Jews in western Europe did not take such an idea seriously. Many of them, emancipated by eighteenth-century Enlightenment ideas, had become successfully integrated into their societies and were comfortable where they were. By the 1880s, however, both western and eastern European Jews were beginning to be ready for this idea. Leo Pinsker advanced a proposal for a secular socialist Jewish state in his 1882 book *Auto-Emancipation*. Nathan Birnbaum seems to have been the first to propose the term Zionism for this concept in 1886.

But the real impetus for the Zionist program came from a Viennese journalist, Theodor Herzl, who was shocked by the anti-Semitism demonstrated in the rigged trial and conviction for treason (in 1894 Enlightenment France, of all places) of Alfred Dreyfus, a Jewish officer. Herzl's 1896 book *Der Judenstaat* [*The Jewish State*] proposed that Jews should have their own nation-state. A superlative communicator, Herzl was able to bring the basic concept of Zionism to the attention of the world. The following year, on August 29, the first Zionist Congress met in Basel, Switzerland, with the objective "to create for the Jewish people a home in Palestine secured by public law" and to promote the settlement of Palestine by skilled and professional Jews. Herzl himself was not personally committed to locating the new Jewish state in Palestine and seriously considered such places as the Sinai Peninsula, Kenya, and Cyprus.

Surprisingly, perhaps, there has been some resistance to Zionism from its very inception from the most orthodox elements in Judaism, based for the most part on three arguments: first, that Zionism is a secular movement and would imperil the essentially religious nature of Judaism; second, that the indigenous Jews and Arabs of Palestine have enjoyed a harmonious relationship that would be disrupted by the introduction of European Zionists in large numbers; and last and most importantly, according to Jewish eschatology, a Jewish state must not be established until the Messiah comes to lead it. The proportion of Orthodox Jews who hold to these views is hotly debated; today they appear to be represented mainly by a branch known as Neturei Karta (an Aramaic name meaning "Guardians of the City").

A History of Religious Tolerance

Nowadays, we have grown accustomed to hearing the present situation blamed not on Christian anti-Semitism but on intrinsic hostility between Muslims and Jews. Plenty of hostility has been built up on both sides over the past century, to be sure, but has it always been this way? Serious students, like Karen Armstrong in *Jerusalem*, William L. Cleveland in *A History of the Modern Middle East*, and I.J. Bickerton and C.L. Klausner in *A Concise History of the Arab-Israeli Conflict* are not quick to offer religious intolerance as a fundamental explanation of current events.

According to accounts of the early history of Islam, together with passages from the Quran [the Koran] and Hadith, Muhammad understood himself to be the last in a series of Jewish prophets, including Jesus, and his mission to be to renew the Jewish prophets' mission to Jews, Christians, and the whole world. The Quran uses the term *ahl al-kitab* (People of the Book) more than thirty times, mostly in Surahs 2–5, allotting special status to Jews and Christians as believers in the Torah and the Gospels (and later, when Islam spread to Persia, the term also included the Zoroastrians). Muhammad did reject those Jews who did not accept him as their prophet, and he regarded the Christian belief that Jesus was the son of God to be a form of polytheism. Still, as People of the Book, they were *dhimmis* (to be protected) under Muslim governments if they paid a *jizya* (poll tax).

In practice there was wide variation in the way Muslim authorities interpreted these rules, and instances are sometimes cited where Jews and Christians fared badly in areas ruled by Muslims. There are other cases, however, where Muslims, Jews, and Christians lived at peace together and even created a remarkably unified kind of community. Perhaps the most notable example is the Muslim city of Cordoba in Spain, where both the Jewish philosopher Moses ben Maimon (Maimonides) and the Arabic philosopher ibn Rushd (Averroes) were born and wrote in Arabic—described in the book *The Ornament of the World* by Maria Rosa Menocal.

The name Palestine originally meant "land of the Philistines." From Greek and Roman times, Palestine was often combined administratively with Syria to form Syro-Palestine. After the Ottoman conquest in 1516, most of Palestine was included in the *vilayet* (major administrative unit) of Syria. Much later, at the start of the nineteenth century, a weakened Ottoman Empire, having repeatedly failed to control Persia (now under the Qajar dynasty), was also forced to accept a semi-autonomous Egypt under Muhammad Ali. Among a series of expansionist moves east and south, Egypt captured Palestine west of the Jordan River—the part we now call "Palestine." Egypt held it from 1831 to 1840 before it returned to the Ottoman Empire, with the northern portion in the *vilayet* of Beirut and the southern in the smaller *sanjak* (district or "flag") of Jerusalem.

Between 1854 and 1869, Egypt built the Suez Canal. But in doing so it drove itself into bankruptcy and in 1882 became a British protectorate. Remember that around 1882 events in Russia and western Europe were leading toward the development of a Zionist movement and the start of Jewish immigration into Palestine. From 1882 on, proximity to the canal and to British power was to have a profound influence on Palestinian-Jewish relations.

Jewish Immigration to Palestine Begins

The Yishuv, as the Jewish community in Palestine was called, began small and grew slowly during the years leading up to World War I.

Immigration was funded mainly by a small number of wealthy European Jews, led by the French Baron Edmond de Rothschild, who was not a Zionist himself. Initially the land was owned by a few rich, mainly absentee landlords who lived in or near urban areas and occupied and worked by many poor peasant farmers (*fellahin*, in Arabic).

Usually the *fellahin* were driven off the land so that Jewish immigrants could occupy it. According to Justin McCarthy's *The Population of Palestine: Population, History, and Statistics of the Late Ottoman Period and the Mandate*—the definitive source for such population data—the first *aliyah* continued from 1882 to 1903, by which time about 90,000 acres were purchased, with about twenty villages and 10,000 new settlers, about half of them in the villages. Successive waves of immigrants varied strikingly in their past lifestyles, those from western or eastern Europe being more accustomed to urban or rural environments, respectively. Accordingly, some chose to work the land themselves while others hired back some of the *fellahin*. According to Bickerton and Klausner:

> Initial Arab peasant opposition subsided when the peasants realized that Jewish landowners would maintain the tradition of permitting them to work the land and keep their income. The number of Jewish settlers was too small to have any serious impact upon Arab agriculture, especially in the hill country. Interestingly, public opposition to Zionist settlement was led by the Greek Orthodox Christians of Palestine.

Still other immigrants gave up and emigrated from Palestine. Of the 40,000 new immigrants arriving in the second *aliyah*, between 1904 and 1914 (David Ben-Gurion was one of the leaders of this group), some estimates say that as many as 90 percent found the conditions inhospitable and left. By 1914 there were still only about forty Jewish settlements in Palestine, owning about 100,000 acres. Of this land about 4 percent had been purchased by the Jewish National Fund (established in 1901), a protected source considered Jewish national property. In 1914 the total population of Palestine was about 722,000, of which only about 60,000 or 8 percent were Jews (12,000 in collective farms and villages). This would be a net increase of only 35,000 in 114 years. By contrast, during the same period, the number of Jews in Europe increased from two million to thirteen million. Equally striking is the fact that, while almost three million Jews left Russia between 1880 and 1914, only about 30,000 of them went to Palestine. After World War I, however, a radical change took place.

The British Influence

The British presence in India and the Far East depended increasingly on control of the Suez Canal and the Persian Gulf. When the Ottoman Empire joined Germany at the start of World War I in 1914,

Britain seized the opportunity to strengthen its long-term position in the Middle East by courting support from Jews and especially Arabs, many of whom (though by no means all) had long chafed under Ottoman rule. Over the next three years, three separate policy statements emerged from these efforts, partially contradicting each other. Sir Henry McMahon, the British high commissioner in Egypt, sent a letter in Arabic to Hussain, Sharif of Mecca, on October 24, 1915, in effect offering independence to the Arabs who would support the British war effort.

The following June, under the leadership of Hussain's son Faisal, the Arab Revolt began—a stirringly romanticized version of which is familiar from the film *Lawrence of Arabia*. While General Edmund Henry Hynman Allenby's forces moved north along the Mediterranean coastline, taking Jerusalem by December 1917, Arabs under Faisal and Thomas Edward Lawrence advanced by a parallel course along Allenby's right flank, east of the Jordan River, blowing up portions of the Hejaz railroad between Damascus and Medina, and taking Damascus by October 1918, shortly before an armistice agreement was signed by the Turks. To complicate later relationships, a Jewish spy ring operating in Palestine was very helpful to Allenby's success in taking Jerusalem. Thus the British had a commanding position over this region during the peace negotiations that followed.

The Balfour Declaration

Meanwhile, the British government had been following different tacks in separate discussions with French and Zionist representatives about the postwar disposition of captured lands in the Middle East. In May 1916, the Sykes-Picot Agreement gave France "influence" or outright control over the northern and western areas corresponding roughly to Syria, southeastern Turkey, and the upper Tigris-Euphrates valley of modern Iraq. The area corresponding most closely to modern Palestine would be governed by an "allied condominium." Then on November 2, 1917, Lord Arthur James Balfour, British foreign secretary, wrote to Lord Lionel Walter Rothschild, head of the British Zionist Organization, an influential "declaration" of two essential parts:

1. "His Majesty's Government view with favour the establishment in Palestine of a national home for the Jewish people, and will use their best endeavours to facilitate the achievement of this object."

2. "It being clearly understood that nothing shall be done which may prejudice the civil and religious rights of existing non-Jewish communities in Palestine, or the rights and political status enjoyed by Jews in any other country."

These two statements contained vague language and translation ambiguities that would later be interpreted as contradicting each other or the McMahon letter. It is of historical importance that Chaim

Weizmann, a brilliant Russian chemist and charismatic Zionist leader who worked in London during the war and much later became Israel's first president, played a crucial role in persuading David Lloyd George, Winston Churchill, and others high in the British government to support the Balfour Declaration.

Misunderstandings became apparent as soon as the Paris peace conference began. Looking for a way out, the British asked Faisal and Weizmann to negotiate personally in an effort to find common ground. Despite their own misgivings the two reached tentative agreement, only to find that everyone had underestimated the growing opposition of the local Arab population, now becoming fearful of Zionist expansion. As a result, the peace conference let the British and French settle Middle East divisions. The actual settlement resembled a simplified version of the Sykes-Picot Agreement, with "mandates" to be governed by Britain and France. The French mandate included modern Lebanon and Syria; the British mandate, modern Palestine, "Transjordan" (modern Jordan), and Iraq.

The Jewish Population Grows

Neither Jews nor Arabs were happy with this outcome. Many Zionists were incensed by a ruling that Jewish immigration would not be permitted in Transjordan. This reaction led to the formation of a Jewish military group, which later became the terrorist organization Irgun. Much later outgrowths were the rise of Menachem Begin and the Likud party. Many Arabs likewise felt betrayed by the possibility of an eventual Jewish state within Palestine. With signs of violent resistance beginning to appear among both Jews and Arabs, the British government began to try to manage Jewish population growth by limiting or prohibiting Jewish immigration to Palestine through a series of three "White Papers" in 1922, 1930, and 1939. Winston Churchill, who was colonial secretary in 1922, issued the first of these. Each White Paper was enforced for a time but abandoned when opposition mounted to an unacceptable level.

Actual immigration reflected conditions in Europe with the approach and reality of World War II. Between 1914 and the start of the mandate and the end of the third *aliyah* (1922), there were 30,000 new immigrants. In the short space of the next fifteen years, the population of Palestine increased by almost 600,000:

	Jews	Arabs
1922	93,000 (12 percent)	700,000 (86 percent)
1931	174,000 (16 percent)	865,000 (82 percent)
1936	383,000 (28 percent)	983,000 (71 percent)

This alarmed the Arabs. William Cleveland comments in *A History of the Modern Middle East*, "It is little wonder that in a region of limited agricultural potential, the ownership of arable land became a matter of contention." He concludes:

> The cumulative effect of land transfers, British policy, and Arab notable attitudes was the increasing impoverishment and marginalization of the Palestinian Arab peasantry. Alienated from their own political elite, who seemed to profit from their plight; from the British, who appeared unwilling to prevent their expulsion from the land; and from the Zionists, who were perceived to be at the root of their problems, they expressed their discontent in outbreaks of violence against all three parties.

My account stops here—approximately seventy years ago. Readers may wonder what this story has to do with today's Israeli/Palestinian conflict. As of the 1930s, the state of Israel had not come into existence, and the Palestinians were referred to merely as Arabs. The Holocaust had not yet occurred, nor had squalid Arab refugee camps developed. Yet as can easily be seen, all the troubles of the present situation are latent in the story told thus far.

ONE LAND, TWO PEOPLE: THE BIRTH OF MODERN ISRAEL

J.J. Goldberg and Phil Sudo

Why do Israelis and Arabs continue to fight over the same tiny piece of land? J.J. Goldberg and Phil Sudo attempt to answer this question in the following selection by providing a brief history of the creation of the modern state of Israel. The authors explain that both Jews and Palestinian Arabs have ancient claims on the land surrounding the city of Jerusalem. After the Holocaust, Goldberg and Sudo write, many European Jews relocated to the Middle East and sought to establish their own nation in their original homeland. However, the Palestinians objected to this plan, as did the leaders of the surrounding Arab states. Two major wars followed, the authors relate, from which Israel not only emerged victorious but also conquered far more territory than originally granted to it by the United Nations. Goldberg is a journalist specializing in American Jewish politics. Sudo is a writer whose work appears in periodicals such as *Scholastic Update* and *New York Times Upfront*.

The conflict between Arabs and Israelis has been one of the longest and most complex of the 20th century. It has led to several wars, thousands of deaths, and the deep involvement of the United States and other nations. But at its heart, the dispute is rooted in the strong and ancient claims of two peoples—the Jews and the Palestinians—to a tiny piece of land in the heart of the Middle East. The following primer is designed to answer basic questions about the Arab-Israeli conflict. How did it start? Why has it lasted so long? And what are the obstacles to a lasting peace?

What Are the Roots of the Conflict?

At the center of the conflict are the powerful competing claims of both Jews and Palestinian Arabs to the land known as Israel—claims that date back thousands of years.

Jewish claims originate in biblical times, when a Jewish kingdom,

J.J. Goldberg and Phil Sudo, "One Land, Two People," *Scholastic Update*, vol. 127, September 16, 1994, p. 6. Copyright © 1994 by Scholastic Inc. Reproduced by permission.

centered in Jerusalem, dominated the area. But by 70 A.D., despite the guidance of such powerful rulers as David and Solomon, the Jewish nation had fallen to the Romans, who forced its people off the land. The Jews called their period of wandering without a homeland the Diaspora, from the Greek word for dispersed. Although they settled in countries the world over, Jews prayed for centuries afterward that one day their people would return to Israel.

Meanwhile, Israel—which the Romans called Palestine—came under Arab domination. By the 9th century, the majority of the population were Muslims—followers of the Prophet Muhammad, the founder of Islam—who, like the Jews, considered Jerusalem one of their holiest cities. For the next 10 centuries, Palestine would be under Muslim rule.

In the late 19th century, Jews in Europe—who were suffering under horrendous persecution—began to organize efforts to create a homeland in Palestine. They called their movement Zionism, after Zion, a hill in northeastern Jerusalem that was the center of ancient Israel. By 1910, some 25,000 Jews had moved to Palestine. At first, the local Arabs lived in peace with the new Jewish settlers. But as the number of settlers grew, so did Arab anger and nationalism. The two groups frequently clashed. The stage was set for an enduring conflict.

In November 1917, the British captured Palestine from the Ottoman Empire, which had ruled it since 1517. In 1922, the League of Nations (predecessor of the United Nations) granted Great Britain the job of governing Palestine and helping Zionist settlers build a Jewish national home there.

That same year, Britain cut off the eastern half of Palestine and created a separate country, at first called Transjordan ("Across the Jordan"), and later Jordan. It was ruled by an Arab nobleman from the Arabian peninsula, Abdullah, the grandfather of Jordan's present-day ruler, King Hussein. Britain ruled the rest of Palestine for 25 years, until hostilities between Jewish settlers and Arabs grew too fierce to handle. In 1947, the British handed the matter over to the United Nations (UN).

Meanwhile, thousands of Jews who had survived the Holocaust—Nazi Germany's extermination of European Jews during World War II (1939–45)—sought out Palestine as a refuge. As a result of the Holocaust, world support for the creation of a Jewish homeland increased dramatically. Finally, in November 1947, the UN voted to divide Palestine into two states, one Jewish and one Palestinian Arab. Middle Eastern Arab states quickly rejected the plan, however, insisting that Palestine should become a single Arab country.

Who Started the Present Conflict?

Most Arabs argue that the establishment of Israel created the conflict by bringing foreign settlers into Palestine and dispossessing the original inhabitants. Most Israelis believe the Arabs started the conflict by refusing to accept the creation of Israel and trying to destroy it.

On May 15, 1948, the day after Israel declared its independence, the armies of five Arab states invaded the new nation. After a year of war, Israel held more territory than it had been given by the UN in the first place. The defeated Arab states signed cease-fire agreements, but they refused to sign a peace treaty, claiming that a state of war continued to exist.

As for the Arab state of Palestine set up by the UN, those parts of it not taken by Israel were absorbed into Egypt and Jordan. Palestinian Arabs have called the war "the Catastrophe." Nearly 1 million Palestinians, left without farms or homes, fled Israel in its aftermath. Yet most of them were turned away from other Arab nations and wound up in UN-run refugee camps in the Gaza Strip and on the West Bank.

What Are the "Occupied Territories"?

In June 1967, Egypt and Syria suddenly mobilized their armies on Israel's borders. Fearing an attack, Israel launched a surprise attack of its own. The next day, King Hussein of Jordan joined the war to help his fellow Arabs.

Over the next six days, Israel defeated all three armies and captured large stretches of their land. From Egypt, Israel won the Sinai Peninsula and Gaza Strip. From Syria, it captured the Golan Heights, a plateau overlooking Israel's northern valleys. From Jordan, Israel took the West Bank, a hilly region of farming villages that formed the heart of ancient Israel and was to have been the center of the Palestinian state in 1948. In winning the West Bank, Israel acquired most of historic Israel, including such emotionally charged places as Bethlehem, Hebron, and the Old City of Jerusalem.

After the war, Israel announced that all territories except Jerusalem would be returned as part of an overall peace agreement. The Arabs, however, refused to negotiate. That November, the UN passed Security Council Resolution 242. It called on Israel to withdraw from the occupied territories in return for "secure and recognized boundaries." The resolution was rejected by the Arabs. But as time went on, most Arab nations came to accept 242 as the basis for today's peace agreements.

Why Is Jerusalem So Crucial?

Jerusalem is the most prized territory in the dispute because it is so steeped in religious history. Jews, Christians, and Muslims all consider the city sacred, and the Old City contains some of the holiest sites in all three religions.

Jewish attachment to Jerusalem dates from 1000 B.C., when King David established the city as the capital of the Israelite tribes. Later, David's son Solomon built the first Temple of the Jews there. Today, the last remnant of Solomon's temple, the Western Wall, stands as Judaism's holiest shrine.

For Christians, Jerusalem is the city where Christ was crucified and buried. The Church of the Holy Sepulcher stands on what is believed to be the hill where Christ carried His cross.

Muslims consider Jerusalem sacred because, in the Islamic faith, it is the site from which Muhammad is believed to have risen to heaven to speak with God. That spot is marked by the golden Dome of the Rock, next to the Western Wall.

The present conflict over Jerusalem dates from the UN partition plan in 1947. The plan called for Jerusalem to be an international city under UN control. But in the 1948 war that followed, Israel captured West Jerusalem, and Jordan held East Jerusalem, including the Old City.

The city stood divided until the Six Day War in 1967, when Israel captured East Jerusalem from Jordan. Since then, Israel has considered the entire city to be its capital, although other nations have refused to recognize Israel's control of the eastern half.

Any hope for a lasting peace, experts say, rides on solving the issue of Jerusalem. Israeli leaders say that an undivided Jerusalem must forever be the capital of Israel, while Palestinians insist that Jerusalem must be the capital of an eventual homeland.

THE TROUBLED HISTORY OF THE OCCUPIED TERRITORIES

Ruth Margolies Beitler

International relations and foreign policy writer Ruth Margolies Beitler examines the history of the Gaza Strip and the West Bank in the following excerpt from the book History Behind the Headlines: The Origins of Conflicts Worldwide. As Beitler relates, when the United Nations decided to partition Palestine into two separate nations in 1947, the Gaza Strip and the West Bank were reserved for the Palestinians. These territories were lost to Jordan and Egypt during the first Arab-Israeli war in 1948, she explains, leaving the Palestinians without a state. During the Six-Day War in 1967, the Israelis captured the Gaza Strip and the West Bank, and they have controlled the two territories ever since. Much of the current conflict between the Israelis and the Arabs centers around the issue of Israel's occupation of these regions, Beitler concludes.

The history of the Palestinian-Israeli conflict is complex and includes many different political forces. The hostility between the Israelis and Palestinians has its roots in the claim by two different national groups to the same territory. In the nineteenth century, Jewish groups, known as Zionists, emerged, advocating a Jewish state in the biblical land of Israel. At the same time, in the Middle East, with the decline of the Ottoman Empire (the Turkish empire that ended in the 1920s), a movement toward a distinct Arab identity was growing. This Arab nationalism competed with political Zionism and led to the increasingly violent conflict between the two groups for statehood in Palestine. The Jews claimed historical, biblical and ideological connections to the land, while Palestinian Arabs attributed their right to Palestine to continued habitation in the land for hundreds of years, along with promises—from Britain and the other major powers—for Arab independence after World War I. The potency of these historical and emotional connections has created one of the most complex questions of the twentieth century.

During the late nineteenth century many Jews began to immigrate

Ruth Margolies Beitler, *History Behind the Headlines: The Origins of Conflicts Worldwide*, vol. 1. New York: Gale Group, 2001. Copyright © 2001 by The Gale Group. Reproduced by permission.

to Palestine, primarily because of growing anti-Semitism—anti-Jewish sentiment—in Europe. Mass attacks on Jews in Russia in the early 1880s forced many to leave their homes in Europe in search of new, more peaceful lives. The majority of emigrants went to the United States, while those Jews with strong religious and nationalist feelings to Palestine, a small area in the Middle East. Once in Palestine, the Jews began to build a strong community with political, social and military institutions. They were preparing to form a state.

Although some Arabs were apprehensive about the number of Jews entering Palestine at the end of the nineteenth century, the Arabs were not necessarily anti-Zionist. They were more concerned about the economic implications of the growing influx of Jews. Yet the situation worsened in 1917 with the proclamation of the Balfour Declaration by the British. The declaration stated that the British monarch "views with favor the establishment in Palestine of a national home for the Jewish people." The Arabs within Palestine felt betrayed.

Prior to this declaration, the British had made a deal with the Arabs regarding Palestine. In communications with the Arabs, the British promised to support their request for independence after WWI if the Arabs agreed to help the British defeat the Ottomans, who had sided with Germany. These letters, which were written between July 1915 and January 1916, became known as the Husayn-McMahon correspondences. The British left the boundaries of the region guaranteed to the Arabs deliberately ambiguous. As such, both the Arabs and Jews believe that they were promised statehood in the same territory. Simultaneously, the British were negotiating a deal with the French called the Sykes-Picot agreement. The agreement defined the areas that would be under French and British control after the war. These included areas both the Arabs and Jews believed the British pledged to them. All of these arrangements conflicted with one another and continue to play a large role in the tensions that remain today.

As expected, with the end of World War I, the San Remo Peace Conference of 1920 created a series of mandates designating that Britain would control Palestine (modern day Israel), Transjordan (modern day Jordan) and Mesopotamia (modern day Iraq). The French received control of Lebanon and Syria. Since their agreement with the Arabs was vague, the British claimed that the area did not include Palestine. The Arabs interpreted the bargain differently. The British could not keep their promises to all groups, but managed to appease the Arabs by creating the modern states of Jordan and Iraq with Arabs in control.

It was only after the Balfour Declaration in 1917 that a distinct Palestinian nationalism began to develop. Previously, the Arabs who lived in Palestine considered themselves an inseparable part of the Arab community, while simultaneously maintaining a special connection to the territory in which they resided. During the early twentieth century, the people of the Middle East were unfamiliar with the modern state concept. Because of this fact, it is not peculiar that neither a strong nor distinctly separate Palestinian identity existed at this time. They viewed themselves as part of the larger Arab community.

As more Jews immigrated to Palestine, the enmity between the Arabs and Jews grew, as did a separate Palestinian identity. As Jewish immigration continued to climb, larger and more violent protests and riots began to occur in Palestine. Despite the increasing hostilities, the Zionists continued to build a political, economic, and military infrastructure in preparation for statehood. The Arabs, on the other hand, chose not to cooperate with the mandatory power and felt that violence could rid the areas of both the Jews and the British. By 1947 the British could no longer contain the fighting between the Arabs and Jews in the territory under their control. Therefore, the British decided to let the United Nations decide who should have the territory. On November 29, 1947, the U.N. General Assembly voted to accept a partition of Palestine. Both the Palestinian Arabs and Jews received territory in which to create two separate states.

The partition of Palestine by the United Nations in 1947 was an attempt by the international community to alleviate the tensions between the two groups. This U.N. action, however, only heightened the level of violence in the region. The Arabs flatly rejected the proposal to create two states, while the Jews reluctantly accepted the U.N.'s decision. Notwithstanding repeated Arab threats to declare war on the Jews if a Jewish state was erected, David Ben-Gurion proclaimed the creation of the state of Israel on May 14, 1948 and became the nation's first Prime Minister. The following day, the first of many Arab-Israeli wars began.

The First Arab-Israeli War

The Palestinians attempted to capture all of Palestine. However, during the 1948 war following the formation of Israel, Israel conquered territory that had been allotted to the Palestinians by the U.N. partition. Additionally, both Jordan (Transjordan) and Egypt took control of areas that had been given to the Palestinians. Jordan gained the West Bank and Egypt administered the Gaza Strip. Thus, the 1948 war left the Palestinians with no state of Palestine as they had been promised in the U.N. partition. At the time, the Palestinians expected the Arab states to help retrieve the land allotted to them by the U.N. Instead, the other Arab states took the land from them.

This shift in control by Jordan and Egypt of the border of the new state of Israel left Israel with three specific security challenges. First, the area of the West Bank that Jordan occupied almost cut Israel in half. The fact that Israel was only ten miles wide at its narrowest point caused considerable concern for the country's security. This security issue continues to be a crucial factor in the current negotiations between the Israelis and Palestinians. Second, the Syrians controlled the strategic position of the Golan Heights. Domination of this area allowed Syria easy access to bomb the Israeli settlements below. Third, Israel acquired a very long border with the Egyptians, along the Sinai desert. Israel was concerned that if the Egyptians massed troops on the border, they could cut Israel off from Eilat, its Red Sea port. The Israelis viewed each of these problems as serious threats to their existence.

The early history provides crucial background for understanding the claims of both the Palestinians and Israelis today. It is also important for grasping the difficulty in finding agreements acceptable to both sides. For example, in 1948 many Palestinians were either forced to leave the newly declared Israeli state or they fled from Israel in fear. Many escaped to the West Bank and Gaza Strip. This exit of Palestinians led to a significant refugee problem. One of the most complex issues in the current Palestinian-Israeli negotiations concerns the fate of these refugees. The region being negotiated for a Palestinian state, however, deals only with the West Bank and Gaza Strip. Many of the refugees left what is today Israel proper. This land is not part of the negotiations for a Palestinian state. With the current peace process, these refugees will have to relinquish their dream of returning to their homes.

The Suez Crisis of 1956

Tensions continued after the 1948 war. Palestinian groups attacked Israel from both the West Bank and Gaza Strip. The Israelis retaliated by bombing both Jordan and Egypt, the states that controlled these areas. By 1956, Israel wanted to stop the infiltration into Israel from the Gaza Strip. During the same period, the British and French worried about Egypt's nationalization of the Suez Canal. (In July 1956 Egypt took control of the Suez Canal—an important waterway for trade and military activity.) For the British, nationalization meant a significant decrease of influence in this strategically important area. Therefore, Israel—in cooperation with the British and French—attacked Egypt on the Sinai Peninsula. Although Israel's attack was successful militarily, the U.S. forced the British and French to stop the attack and demanded that Israel pull out of the Sinai and Gaza Strip. The military was forced to withdraw from the Gaza Strip and a small U.N. force was stationed there to monitor the activities of Israel and Egypt. Throughout the Arab world, and especially in Egypt, Egyptian president Gamal Abd al-Nasser was seen as standing up to the Western forces.

Following the Suez war of 1956, the Palestinians relied on other Arab countries to get the land back from Israel. Since Nasser had stood up to the West, the Palestinians hoped that soon Palestine would return to their control. At this stage in the conflict, the Arab states and the Palestinians were interested in destroying Israel and regaining all of Palestine, not just the area allotted to the Palestinians by the U.N. partition.

The Creation of the PLO

While the Egyptians controlled the Gaza Strip, they wanted to curtail Palestinian guerrilla attacks from Gaza. The Egyptians knew that Israel would not hesitate to retaliate for guerrilla attacks by attacking Egyptian territory. Since the Arab states were unable to control the Palestinian guerrilla groups, the Arab states created the Palestinian Liberation Organization (PLO) in 1964. The Egyptians, the main proponent of this organization, believed that the creation of the PLO would allow them some control over Palestinian activities. Egypt hoped the PLO would unify the various guerrilla groups under this new umbrella organization, uniting all Palestinians, wherever they were located.

One of the groups that Egypt wanted to control was Fatah, an organization founded in the late 1950's by students in Cairo. Fatah became one of the main branches of the PLO. Yasir Arafat, who was involved in Fatah's creation, is currently the president of the Palestinian Authority in the West Bank and Gaza Strip.

By 1965 Fatah was frustrated with the Arab states' reluctance to take immediate action regarding the call for an all-out battle to destroy Israel. The Palestinians tried to lure the Arab states into war with Israel by continuing their guerrilla attacks on Israel, relying on Israel to strike back. However, after the Suez crisis, even though Egyptian president Nasser had stood up to the West, he recognized the enormous military power of the Israelis. He was not interested in being drawn into a conflict with Israel until he was prepared. Unfortunately, Nasser made a series of moves that Israel viewed as hostile, including closing the Gulf of Aqaba to Israeli shipping and removing U.N. forces from Egyptian soil. Believing itself threatened, Israel attacked Egypt in what Israel claimed was a preemptive strike—attacking Egypt before Egypt could attack Israel. The Arab states believed that it was an unprovoked attack.

During the Six-Day War, Israel fought Egypt, Jordan and Syria. As in 1948, the end of the Six-Day War left the Israelis in control of more Arab territory. The Arab states' defeat during the Six-Day War resolved several problems for Israel while creating others. Israel's acquisition of the Golan Heights, the Sinai Desert, the West Bank and Gaza Strip produced more secure borders for Israel. Yet the capture of the West Bank and Gaza Strip left Israel in control of 1.3 million Palestinians who were hostile to the notion of Israeli domination. Once the Israelis controlled these areas, the Palestinians and Israelis were in daily contact in both the territories and in Israel proper. This increased contact fashioned a very different relationship than the one between the Arab states and Israel.

Furthermore, the present negotiations discussing the delineation of borders for a Palestinian entity or state are closely linked with the results of the Six-Day War. Many Palestinians in the West Bank and Gaza Strip advocated their independent state have the borders that existed prior to the 1967 war—the Palestinians want a state comprised of the West Bank and Gaza Strip. After the 1967 war, the U.N. passed Resolution 242 calling for "withdrawal from territories occupied in the recent conflict." Acceptance of the resolution implied acceptance of the concept of "land for peace"—giving up control of the land in exchange for peaceful coexistence. In addition, the resolution called for the recognition of the "sovereignty, territorial integrity and political independence of every state in the area." This suggested a mutual recognition by the Israelis and Palestinians. This mutual recognition did not occur until 1993.

By gaining control of the West Bank in 1967, the Israelis also attained control of all of Jerusalem. Prior to the Six-Day War, Jerusalem was under Jordanian rule. During that period, Jews were not permitted to visit their holy sites, particularly the Western Wall. Once the Israelis captured the city, the Jews vowed never to let it be divided again. The Israelis have allowed open access to all holy sites. The issue of Jerusalem is one of the most difficult issues that the Palestinians and Israelis must negotiate. Both groups claim Jerusalem as their capital and want full control of their sacred places.

An overwhelming change in the Palestinians' philosophy and tactics occurred after the horrible defeat of the Arab armies during the Six-Day War. It was following this stunning debacle that the Palestinians recognized the need to discover a more effective strategy to gain independence. The conflict then shifted from one between the Arab states and Israel to a separate one between the West Bank and Gaza Strip inhabitants and the Israelis.

The 1973 War (Yom Kippur War)

In 1973, by executing a surprise attack, the Arab states made an attempt to defeat the Israelis and retrieve the land lost during the Six-Day War. Although the Arab states inflicted severe casualties on the Israelis, they were unable to regain control of Israeli-held territories. To put an end to the hostilities, the U.N. passed Resolution 338 that specified direct negotiations between the parties involved to implement Resolution 242.

The war in 1973 again convinced the Palestinians that they could not depend on the Arab states to liberate their land. Moreover, the PLO was becoming increasingly interested in pursuing both diplomatic and military strategies. Real movement toward an Israeli-Palestinian agreement, however, did not occur until the uprising in the Gaza Strip and West Bank in 1987.

The Palestinian uprising in the Gaza Strip and West Bank, also known as the Intifada, reflected a changed Palestine. The Palestinians within the territories were ready to take matters into their own hands to create an independent Palestinian state. The outbreak of violent demonstrations and riots in December 1987 had several causes. After

20 years of Israeli control of the West Bank and Gaza Strip, Palestinian frustration peaked. Many had grown up under Israeli control and had never experienced democratic freedoms. The increased contact with the Israeli population because of employment opportunities in Israel proper allowed the Palestinians to view a different lifestyle. Additionally, the improved standard of living as a result of higher wages in Israel without a corresponding increase of political and social freedom escalated the Palestinians' frustration. The growth of a more educated Palestinian population also heightened many Palestinians' expectations for better opportunities and civil rights.

Furthermore, the Palestinians became severely dependent on Israel due to the lack of an economic infrastructure. This dependence increased both the population's frustration and hastened the growth of a strong Palestinian national identity, one separate from being Arab. The development of a potent national identity was crucial in influencing the eruption of the Intifada.

Another factor that led to increased hostilities in the territories was the war in 1973. It was viewed in the Arab world as a victory. The Arab states were able to launch a surprise assault on Israel and inflict a large number of casualties. In the eyes of the Arabs, especially the Palestinians, Israel's deterrent power was waning.

President Anwar Sadat of Egypt made an historic visit to Jerusalem in 1977. In 1978 President Sadat and Israeli president Menachem Begin signed the Camp David Accords, which secured peace between Egypt and Israel in exchange for Israel returning the Sinai desert. This event had a profound effect on the Palestinians. The Palestinians had assumed that any peace treaty with an Arab state would contain a comprehensive agreement for a Palestinian state. The Palestinians expected the Egyptians to force the Israelis to return the West Bank and Gaza Strip as part of any peace deal. Sadat attempted to maintain the connection between the return of the Sinai with the Palestinian state, but he was unsuccessful; once again, the West Bank and Gaza Strip were brushed aside. The Palestinians, frustrated by both Israeli actions and those of their Arab brethren, sought a path with which to push the issue of their statehood back into the foreground.

One of the most controversial issues and a large contributor to the Intifada in 1987 was Israel's settlement policy. When the Likud, Israel's center-right party, assumed power in 1977, its policies were based on the ideology of Greater Israel. This meant that retaining parts of the biblical land of Israel was a key political platform. The Likud was more interested in holding onto territory than in conducting a peace process. Many Israelis contended that settlements would provide added protection for Israel; consequently, Jews moved into the Arab portions of Israeli-held territory and established towns. The new Jewish communities, however, only incited resentment among the Arabs.

From 1977–87, many settlements were established close to Arab villages. Prior to 1977, the Jewish settlements were relatively isolated from the Arab areas. Until the Likud Party's defeat in 1992, the settlement policy continued to incite anger. Some academics argued that the policy was not shortsighted, but was implemented precisely to gain permanent control of the region.

Israel created policies to control the inhabitants, including deportations. These policies contributed to the inability of the moderate West Bank or Gaza Strip Palestinians to establish a political party to negotiate with the Israelis. While the Israelis did not grant Palestinians freedom of political activity on the West Bank and Gaza, the PLO also refused to permit the West Bank Palestinians to found an independent political party. Yasir Arafat's major interest was to prevent the emergence of an independent Palestinian leadership in the territories. The PLO feared that any separate authority would diminish its power and legitimacy as the "sole representative" of the Palestinian people. Because many Palestinians were scattered in other countries, the PLO wanted to maintain its influence over matters concerning *all* Palestinians. Therefore, the existence of the Intifada indicated a rift between the Palestinians in the territories and the external Palestinian leadership.

Because of Palestinian frustration with Arafat and the PLO for not being able to deliver on their promises of liberating Palestine or at least in making progress diplomatically, the West Bank and Gaza Strip Palestinians concluded that they should act independently. The Intifada, however, was not a well-thought-out, calculated event. The uprising was a spontaneous reaction to specific triggering events including an incident during which a Palestinian terrorist crossed the Israeli border using a hang-glider, entered an army base in northern Israel, and killed six soldiers. This action was a victory for the terrorists and proved that the great Israeli army, which had dealt the conventional Arab armies a devastating blow in 1967, was vulnerable.

Thus, there were several factors that led to the outbreak of violent demonstrations and riots in December 1987. The Intifada forced the policy makers to reevaluate Israel's objectives within the territories. The Intifada reflected a new self-reliance for the Palestinians in the occupied territories. They no longer trusted the other Arab states or Palestinians from outside the territories to retrieve the land promised to them by the U.N. in 1947.

Furthermore, during the Intifada Israel frequently sealed the territories to contain protesters and did not allow the Palestinians access to their jobs in Israel. As such, they were forced to become more self-sufficient. When the Palestinians could not work, their anger increased. The Israelis realized that they could not continue to control the occupied territories without great cost.

THE OSLO ACCORDS AND THE DEMISE OF THE PEACE PROCESS

Baylis Thomas

In the following excerpt from his book *How Israel Was Won: A Concise History of the Arab-Israeli Conflict*, Baylis Thomas recounts the events surrounding the Oslo Peace Accords of 1993. Although the accords were hailed as an important step toward creating peace between Israel and the Palestinians, Thomas reports that there was dissatisfaction on both sides. Many Palestinians felt Yasser Arafat, the leader of the Palestine Liberation Organization, had given away too much, he explains, while many Israelis likewise felt that Prime Minister Yitzhak Rabin had made too many concessions. The peace process initiated by the Oslo accords faltered in November 1995, when Rabin was assassinated by an orthodox Jewish extremist who opposed Israel's negotiations with the Palestinians. Thomas describes the escalation of violence that took place after Rabin's assassination as Arafat and the new Israeli prime minister, Benjamin Netanyahu, repeatedly clashed. Thomas is a freelance journalist and clinical psychologist who specializes in examining the sources of individual and group conflicts.

The Gulf War demonstrated that Israel's security lay in technological defense against missile attack from distant soils, not in acquiring more land in the immediate vicinity (i.e., the West Bank). Nevertheless, after the war, Israel continued spending billions of dollars for expropriation and settlement of the occupied territories in the name of security, infuriating President George Bush and his secretary of state James Baker. Prime Minister Yitzhak Shamir demanded $10 billion from the United States for even more settlements but Bush faced him down.

Secretary Baker attempted to control settlement expansion by sponsoring talks among Israel, the Arab states and Palestinians (a non-PLO delegation, including Hanan Ashwari, Faisal Husseini and Rashid Khalidi) dealing with interim forms of autonomy in the occupied territories. Ten international conferences (the "Madrid Confer-

Baylis Thomas, *How Israel Was Won: A Concise History of the Arab-Israeli Conflict*. Lanham, MD: Lexington Books, 1999. Copyright © 1999 by Lexington Books. Reproduced by permission.

ences") were held between late 1991 and the middle of 1993. In the midst of these talks, a Rabin/Labor government was elected on a platform promising peace with the Palestinians in a year.

Yet [Prime Minister Yitzhak] Rabin remained Israel's tough "security man" concerning the territories. As he put it, "Security takes precedence over peace"—that is, control takes precedence over negotiation. In pursuit of that control over the occupied territories, Rabin devoted large sums for "strategic settlements" in "security areas" comprising about one-half of the West Bank, with $600 million spent on construction of interconnecting roads in 1994. The prime minister also authorized the continued construction of 10,000 housing units for Jews only in the Arab–East Jerusalem section of the West Bank. By these actions Rabin brought the Madrid talks to a point of crisis in November 1992. The Palestinians were outraged, claiming that Israel would effectively control two-thirds of the West Bank. Then, in early 1993, Rabin deported 416 alleged Hamas activists—an act that discredited the talks and galvanized Palestinian extremists. Thirteen Israelis were murdered a month later by terrorists and Rabin completely sealed off Israel from the occupied territories.

The Oslo Peace Accords

Initially, Rabin had little interest in some informal, secret, Jewish-Palestinian talks taking place in Oslo. But after the Madrid talks collapsed, Rabin had greater need to find a way to fulfill his campaign pledge of peace. Moreover, talks with Syria about conditions for Israeli withdrawal from the Golan Heights—a strategy proposed by Ehud Barak (Israeli Defense Force [IDF] Chief of Staff) to draw the Arab countries together in order to isolate and weaken the bargaining power of Palestinians—had gone nowhere. There were other reasons why Rabin reconsidered the Oslo talks. Yasir Arafat, the key, was personally in a weak position. His declaration of a Palestinian state had been ignored by the West and he was persona non grata with President Bush. He had also lost the support of the collapsing Soviet Union and had provoked the anger of Saudi Arabia over his position on the Gulf War. Rabin saw that Arafat was at serious disadvantage as a negotiator and that the Palestinians, exhausted by the intifada, might now be willing to come to favorable terms. "It became clear that the PLO was bankrupt, divided and on the verge of collapse and therefore ready to settle for considerably less," [according to historian Avi Shlaim].

Rabin threw Arafat a life line with little risk to himself and potential gain for Israeli security—Arafat's secular PLO might conceivably be able to suppress Islamic terror groups. After eight months of secret talks, an agreement was reached—the *Oslo Peace Accords*.

What the United States called a "historic breakthrough," Palestine National Council (PNC) member Edward Said called "a Palestinian

Versailles" and Israel's Amos Oz characterized as "the second biggest victory in the history of Zionism." On the surface, the Oslo Accords looked benignly helpful to the Palestinian cause regarding self-determination. Agreed upon was the "Declaration of Principles on Interim Self-Government Arrangements" (DOP). This was not so much a set of agreements as an *agenda* for negotiations. However, some things were agreed: There was to be a *transfer of power* to Palestinians for an *interim* period. Palestinians would be permitted to administer unto themselves in five spheres: health, social welfare, direct taxation, education/culture and tourism. After two months, Israel would withdraw from Gaza and Jericho, redeploying troops to surrounding areas. The PLO would train a police force for local, internal Palestinian security though Israel would remain responsible for overall security in the West Bank and Gaza. It was also agreed that within nine months, a *Palestinian Council* would be elected by Palestinians to take over administrative functions for the PLO. Within two years, discussions would begin concerning a *permanent* settlement to be enacted in five years, a settlement separate from any agreements made during the interim period.

For the Palestinians, exhausted by the intifada and brutalized by the occupation, the idea of gaining even limited autonomy with partial IDF withdrawal was a cause for celebration. On the other hand, for Palestinian leaders outside the Arafat camp—for example, Dr. 'Abd al-Shafi, a Madrid negotiator, and PNC member Edward Said—the primary disappointment of the Oslo Accords was their failure to address the fundamental issue of Palestinian *sovereignty* over the West Bank and Gaza. Palestinian territorial rights were never mentioned, even as a negotiable item on the agenda. Nor did the Accords place any restrictions on the continued building of Jewish settlements and their interconnecting road networks—that is, further erosion of Palestinian territory (some 65 percent of the West Bank already under Israeli control).

Clearly, the Accords were possible only because negotiations about all the difficult and important issues relating to the Israeli-Palestinian conflict were excluded. Sovereignty, Jewish settlements, Palestinian refugee return and East Jerusalem were all off-limits. Rather, the central focus of the Oslo Accords was on the *security of Jewish settlements and Israel* and the requirement that the PLO suppress Islamic militants as a precondition for withdrawal of Israeli troops from certain Palestinian areas.

The Recognition Letters

The most important feature of the Oslo Accords, for detractors and supporters alike, was not the DOP provisions for limited autonomy/ self-rule, but the *preamble letters* that conferred mutual recognition on the PLO and Israel. Nabil Shaath, Arafat's close advisor and negotiator, found in these recognition letters a parity between the two sides.

Said saw the opposite—no parity where Palestinians had no power from which to negotiate, where "mutual" recognition was really *unilateral* recognition.

It is true that in this exchange of letters Arafat gave away much, Rabin little. Arafat affirmed: (1) PLO recognition of Israel's right to exist in peace and security; (2) renunciation of the Palestinian Covenant; (3) acceptance of UN Resolutions 242 and 338 (despite their omission of Palestinian territorial rights); (4) renunciation of the use of terrorism and other acts of violence; and (5) assumption of overall responsibility for the behavior of PLO elements and personnel. In exchange, Rabin gave to Arafat recognition that the PLO represented the Palestinian people with whom Israel would negotiate. That is, Arafat recognized both the Jewish State and its right to security while Rabin recognized Arafat as an agent for a collection of people without a state or a similar right to security. Ignored outright was the Palestinian state declared five years earlier and recognized by over 100 countries—a nullity in the Accords.

Palestinian Critiques of the Accords

Arafat's recognition of Israel had, in the opinion of some Palestinian scholars, given away, wittingly or unwittingly, explicitly or implicitly, a number of important and fundamental Palestinian legal rights:

(1) Arafat's recognition of and agreements with Israel constituted an admission that Israel *rightfully* possessed powers in the territories which it was empowered or entitled, through the Oslo Accords, to *transfer*, at its discretion, to the Palestinians. Such right of power does conflict with accepted international opinion concerning Israel's legal status as an occupier of conquered territories—occupiers do not possess powers which they can legally transfer to the occupied. If Israel had practiced *de facto* sovereignty over the territories since 1967, Arafat now seemed to be conferring on Israel *de jure* sovereignty. In this respect, Israel became the rightful possessor of powers, some of which Arafat hoped might be transferred to the Palestinians. "We have," declared 'Abd al-Shafi, "helped to confer legitimacy on what Israel has established illegally."

(2) Arafat's admission of Israeli rights and powers in the territories also seemed to have the effect of undermining the Palestinians' right of appeal to international courts for protection normally afforded people under occupation. Such protections include the Fourth Geneva Conventions, the Hague Conventions and other international laws prohibiting use of life-threatening force and torture, prohibiting settlement of occupied territories, etc.—conventions and laws systematically violated in the territories before and after the Accords. To cast off occupier status seemed to undermine the occupied's right to international appeal.

(3) Another criticism of the Accords was that recognition of Israel

constituted a recognition of Israel's *laws*, including martial law in the territories. These laws, still in force, have in fact led to expropriation of land and water, imposition of taxes and deportation of inhabitants.

(4) The clause about Israel's "right to exist in peace and security" has also been construed as an Israeli right to remedy any situation it deems threatening to security—for example, reintroduction of troops or undercover agents into self-rule areas to handle settler-Palestinian conflicts or apprehend suspected terrorists.

(5) But the central Palestinian criticism of the Oslo Accords involved Arafat's commitment to Israel's peace and security. This commitment made him responsible for Palestinian terrorism, future intifadas or other violence directed at Israelis. Israel assumed no parallel responsibility for IDF or settler violence directed at Palestinians. Moreover, Arafat's pledge to end violence set him squarely against Hamas and Islamic Jihad, thereby creating conditions for a potential civil war within the Palestinian community. As historian Avi Shlaim noted, this was a Rabin strategy "aimed at playing the Arabs off one against the other in order to reduce the pressure on Israel to make concessions."

With Arafat "on the ropes" (as Rabin appraised) and Hamas "flourishing" (as Israeli intelligence reported), it was unlikely that Arafat could accomplish what Israel had not during the previous six years— suppression of dissident Islamic terrorists. Certainly, suicide bombings would be impossible to prevent. Consequently, Rabin had available to him seemingly justified grounds for halting negotiations whenever Ararat failed (predictably) to fulfill his commitment to Israeli security. Moreover, given Israel's continuing land expropriation, exclusion of Palestinian labor from Israel, collective punishment and Shin Bet (Secret Service) operations in the Palestinian police, Arafat's chance of suppressing dissident Palestinian terrorism could only worsen.

Rabin's Goals

What was Rabin's ultimate goal in signing the Oslo Accords? Was he, like Shamir, toying with Palestinians in endless talk about autonomy while confiscating land in the cause of Greater Israel—maintaining the status quo? Or seeking the *appearance* of peacemaker without much risk or cost? Or was he seeking to shift responsibility for terrorism onto Arafat to discredit him? Did he actually think that Arafat could deliver on Israel's security?

Certainly Rabin was following Shamir's classic fait accompli strategy of expansion in the West Bank and, like Shamir, avoiding the issue of Palestinian sovereignty. And yet Rabin did *not* want to incorporate two million West Bank and Gazan Palestinians into Israel by annexing the occupied territories. He once favored the 1967 Allon Plan whereby Israel would annex Jewish settlement areas and the Jordan Valley (eastern side of the West Bank) but not the densely populated Palestinian areas better controlled by Jordan—the once-popular

"Jordanian option." Certainly, he and the Israeli public wanted to be rid of the Gaza Strip, a sealed-off, packed prison of angry unemployed Palestinians that, in his view, might best "sink into the sea." Turning responsibility for the Gaza Strip over to the PLO was certainly one of Rabin's goals. Hence, the defensible conclusion of Israeli researcher Meron Benvenisti that Oslo was a device to enable the Israelis to gradually evacuate "precisely those [dense Palestinian population areas] they were keen to get rid of." In any event, Arafat accepted the Gaza offer and, needing to show Palestinians that he could bargain for a foothold and symbolic concession in the West Bank, demanded and received Jericho as well.

But Rabin's goal may finally have been one of *separation*, in which West Bank Palestinians were to end up in a dozen, small, densely populated "self-rule" enclaves militarily encircled and effectively walled off from Israel. This plan, described below, was announced in January of 1995, the year of Rabin's assassination.

In sum, Rabin accomplished through the Oslo Accords a number of goals on the main issues: (1) PLO recognition of Israel's power and ultimate security responsibilities over all the occupied territories; (2) PLO acquiescence to continued settlement-building on rapidly diminishing amounts of land, (3) PLO responsibility for halting Palestinian terrorism and suicide bombings; and (4) PLO responsibility for the Gaza Strip. The rest of the Accords concerned protracted negotiations over secondary issues about the exact timing, meaning and extent of limited Palestinian autonomy.

Oslo II

Two years after the 1993 Oslo Accords when the Palestinians were on their own (their former guardian, Jordan, had signed a peace treaty with Israel in 1994), the Palestinians and Israelis made further interim agreements. Dubbed "Oslo II," or the Taba agreements, these agreements were designed to slowly extend Palestinian self-rule to other towns and villages besides Gaza and Jericho. This plan, if and when completed, was to give administrative and police control (not sovereignty) to Palestinians over about 3 percent of the West Bank (called Area A). Another 24 percent (Area B) was to have a Palestinian administration with joint Israeli/Palestinian military control. The remaining 73 percent, comprising Israeli "public" lands, settlements, army camps and roads, was to remain under exclusive Israeli control. Hebron, a city of 120,000 Palestinians and 400 Israelis, posed a special case in which Israel was to retain part control of the city. The accords also allowed for construction of a system of internal roadblocks that could prevent north-south Palestinian travel in the West Bank and entry into East Jerusalem.

To summarize the agreements of Oslo I and II: *(a)* Palestinians have administrative authority to control health, social welfare, direct taxation, education/culture, tourism and policing in limited areas of the West Bank and Gaza; *(b)* Israel has responsibility for security over all the West Bank and Gaza and exclusive control of and authority for the security of all Jewish settlements and settlers even when in Palestinian self-rule (A) areas; *(c)* Israel has veto power over all laws drafted by the Palestinian Council; *(d)* Israel's occupier laws remain in force throughout the West Bank and Gaza; *(e)* all Palestinian administrative appointments require Israeli approval; *(f)* Israel has the exclusive power to collect customs fees and to tax locally produced Palestinian goods; *(g)* Israel controls all commercial and personal traffic between Gaza and the West Bank and between the West Bank, Israel and Jordan; and *(h)* Israel controls all exits and entries to Palestinian self-rule areas and controls all roads.

The Faltering Peace Process

As previously described, Arafat's failure to assure Israel's security (a violation of the Oslo Accords) could be expected to threaten self-rule negotiations. On the other hand, were he to successfully suppress Hamas, he would alienate Palestinians sympathetic to Hamas and jeopardize his own political base. Were Arafat more popular his dilemma would be less. But some Palestinians have seen Arafat as a dictator who has merely replaced Israel's military governor. And the PLO has been criticised as a corrupt patronage system in which members indulge in luxurious living amidst the people's poverty. Arafat's strong-armed police force, charged with keeping the peace, has been accused of doing Israel's "dirty work"—torturing and killing Palestinians in pursuit of Islamic dissidents. If Arafat works for Israeli and not Palestinian security, his popular support erodes.

Moreover, Hamas has enjoyed begrudging respect from more than 20 percent of Palestinians. Many have rejected Hamas's terrorist acts and seen its Islamic ideology as intolerant and undemocratic. Yet Hamas has also exhibited concern for the people, delivering food, clothes, money and jobs to poor Palestinians. [As commentator Neil MacFarquhar writes], "Many downtrodden Gazans depend on Hamas charity to feed their children—a consideration for Mr. Arafat if he were to crack down hard as Israel demands." The people, in "existential crisis, demoralized, depoliticized and depressed . . . facing a cavernous void," [according to Norman Finkelstein in *The Rise and Fall of Palestine*] admire the fact that Hamas and Islamic Jihad have at least *acted* against IDF and settler violence.

Arafat's dilemma: he gains a degree of popular support by making progress on Israeli withdrawal, but if that requires open civil war with Hamas and Islamic Jihad, he also loses some support. Hanan Ashrawi believes that, "The more the PLO shows it can deliver on the Israelis' principle demand—security—the less it is accepted by its own people." Israel and Hamas both understand Arafat's bind—they know that it is not as simple as Israel alleges, that Arafat is a terrorist sympathizer, nor as simple as Hamas alleges, that Arafat is an Israeli collaborator.

The Peace Process Is Destroyed

In November 1995, two months after Oslo II, Rabin was assassinated by a Jewish religious fundamentalist, an act dramatizing the intense differences between orthodox and secular groups in Israel. Shimon Peres took over the premiership and called for early elections in the summer of 1996. In a close vote, Peres lost to Likud's Benjamin Netanyahu, who had campaigned on a platform seeking to nullify the "dangerous" Oslo Peace Accords. Terrorist bombings provided an election boost for Netanyahu's no-accommodation position.

Netanyahu has been described [by Serge Schmemann] as having been "waiting all along for a way to get out of an arrangement he always held in disdain." Like Rabin, security has been seen by him as a product of strength rather than peace negotiations and his disdain has been linked not only to a "deep-seated distrust of the Oslo peace agreement [but also] of the Arabs," [Schmemann notes]. Netanyahu's writings suggest a "vision of the Jew as perennial target who can never entrust his security to anyone, who must surround himself with what Vladimir Jabotinsky called a 'steel wall.'"—that making peace with Arabs is like "keeping fish in a glass bowl until they learn not to bump against the glass," [according to Schmemann].

Foreign minister David Levy has criticized the prime minister for "destroying the peace" through actions seemingly designed to scuttle the Accords. These have included: tunnel-building in Jerusalem; a massive housing project at Har Homa; a dam project on Syria's doorstep; the delayed Oslo II deployment of Israeli forces from self-rule areas; the punishment of Palestinians through harsh economic sanctions; the withholding of Palestinian tax monies from the Palestinian Authority; and the sealing off of Israel from Palestinian labor and goods. These actions could be expected to fuel Palestinian anger and only add to Arafat's inability to control terror. Some have wondered whether Netanyahu has been the indirect source of the terrorism that he has used to disparage Palestinians and freeze withdrawal negotiations.

The prime minister did make a concession in early 1997 of withdrawing the IDF from three-quarters of Hebron (virtually an all-Arab town). At the same time, his approval of the rapid expansion of Jewish housing at Har Homa (southern Jerusalem in the West Bank), some 6,500 new units in April 1997, drew condemnation from the UN General Assembly. Netanyahu declared: "We shall build in Jerusalem and everywhere, no one will deter us." He plans to enlarge Jerusalem to half again its current size and build many more Jewish homes in Har Homa by the year 2000 despite U.S. disapproval. Netanyahu has been on the same expansionist track as Rabin and

Peres who together increased settlements by 49 percent during their four-year rule.

Suicide bombings in Jerusalem in the summer of 1997 brought the "peace process" to a halt. Netanyahu refused negotiations about withdrawal and held Arafat responsible. Arafat accused Netanyahu of a "plot to stop and destroy the agreements." Their mutual recriminations involved a circular linkage in which suicide bombings lead to halted negotiations which in turn lead to more suicide bombings. The United States has favored Netanyahu's side: [In January 1997, the U.S. State Department declared that] "Only if the Palestinian side proves itself able and willing to comply with its security responsibilities is Israel obligated to transfer additional areas in the West Bank to Palestinian jurisdiction"—confirmation to the terrorists that bombings are effective in sabotaging negotiations seen as submission to Israel.

Settler violence in the occupied territories worsened after the 1993 Accords. Settlers feared that limited self-rule would compromise what they considered rightful Jewish sovereignty over all of Palestine. Clashes accelerated. A settler massacred twenty-nine Palestinian worshippers in Hebron in February 1994. This was followed by the killing of thirty Arabs by the IDF, ushering in a wave of revenge suicide bombings by Hamas. In January 1997, when settlers in Hebron brandished Uzi sub-machine guns and laid claim to Palestinian land, eight protesting Palestinians were shot by an off-duty IDF soldier. Two months later fifty-eight Palestinians were shot by the IDF during a demonstration over Israeli construction at Har Homa. The Israeli government has been no more able or willing to curb the violence of the IDF, undercover agents or extremist settlers than has Arafat been able or willing to curb Islamic extremists. . . .

Is the Middle East Conflict Over?

Given the future prospects for Palestinians, Palestinian terrorism cannot be expected to end. In that sense, the Middle East conflict is *not* over. As long as any Palestinian is willing to kill an Israeli and himself in protest or frustration over statelessness, injustice and poverty, Israel will have a security problem. And as long as any settler, Shin Bet operative or Israeli soldier is willing to kill a Palestinian for God, country or retaliation, Palestinians will have a security problem. As long as both Palestinians and Jews terrorize and are terrorized by "sacrificers" against injustice and loss, Hamas and [religious Zionist group] Gush Emunim alike, a *mutual* local security problem will remain. Attempts to stop terrorism through infliction of collective punishment or through bestowal of limited self-rule seem to have only fueled the problem. Nor has Israeli assassination of Palestinian figures such as Abu Jihad or Yahya Ayyash accomplished more than provoke counterattack—as when, in March 1996, Hamas ended its self-imposed ceasefire. Palestinian terrorism cannot be punished away any more than could Jewish terrorism be punished away by the British in 1946–1948. "It is not easy to get a conquered person to resign himself to defeat," [as Maxime Rodinson writes in *Israel: A Colonial-Settler State?*] Nor does moral condemnation work. When violence is the last bargaining chip of those feeling oppressed, it elicits little guilt. So as long as local terrorism persists, . . . the Middle East conflict is not over.

SHATTERED HOPES FOR PEACE IN THE NEW CENTURY

Peter Vilbig

In September 2000, hopes for peace between Israelis and Palestinians came closer to reality than ever before. However, explains
Peter Vilbig, misunderstandings and lack of communication
ended up unraveling the peace process. In the following article,
the author traces the events that led to the fresh outbreak of violence, including Israeli opposition party leader Ariel Sharon's
controversial visit to the Temple Mount, which ignited riots that
contributed to derailing the peace negotiations at Camp David.
He also notes that a number of observers—including U.S. president Bill Clinton—felt that Palestinian leader Yasser Arafat
ensured the ultimate failure of the peace talks by refusing to
grant as many concessions as did Israeli prime minister Ehud
Barak. Despite the violence that has plagued the region since the
peace talks broke down, Vilbig relates, many people still believe
that peace, which was so close, can yet be accomplished. Vilbig
writes for *New York Times Upfront* magazine.

Again and again in a year of bloodshed, the pendulum of violence has
ticked from one side to the other. With each swing, someone dies.

On one day, the eerie back-and-forth might begin with young
Palestinians, willing to die as martyrs for their dream of a free Palestine. Carefully, they tape pipe bombs and high explosives to their
bodies and slip into busy Israeli streets. Outside a crowded disco, a
bomber kills himself and 21 others, many of them teens. At a pizza
restaurant, another suicide bomber kills 15 Israeli civilians.

A few hours or days later, the pendulum swings back. A black
Israeli attack helicopter, its rotors chugging in the heated air, rises
over the dry landscape, holds steady for an instant, and then fires its
missiles in a long streak of hissing smoke. Whether the target is an
office building, a farmhouse in Bethlehem, or a lone car on a deserted
road at midnight, the results are the same: The Palestinian militants
who have been marked for extermination end up dead, and sometimes innocent bystanders die too.

Peter Vilbig, "Shattered Hope," *New York Times Upfront*, vol. 134, September 17, 2001,
p. 16. Copyright © 2001 by The New York Times Company and Scholastic Inc.
Reproduced by permission.

It was not supposed to be this way. [In September 2000], the Israelis and Palestinians were said to be close to signing a peace pact, the culmination of seven years of painful negotiations. Then the talks suddenly broke down. Since then, violence has claimed the lives of more than 550 Palestinians and more than 130 Israelis.

Each new attack leads to oaths of vengeance—from Palestinian militants bent on continuing the terror campaign, and from the Israeli Army, which vows to continue targeted killings.

A Wrong Turn

The United States has blamed Palestinian leader Yasir Arafat for the failure. One widely accepted story goes like this: [In the summer of 2000], the two sides met with President Bill Clinton at Camp David, the presidential retreat in Maryland. At that meeting, Ehud Barak, who was then Israel's Prime Minister, offered Arafat a deal too good to refuse. But, the story continues, Arafat turned down the Israeli plan, and then "pushed the button" and chose the path of violence.

However, new details have emerged, suggesting that the version blaming Arafat for the failure of the peace talks was largely wrong. Diplomats and officials now say the reality was far more complex. "It is a terrible myth that Arafat and only Arafat caused this catastrophic failure," says Terje Roed-Larsen, the United Nations special envoy in Jerusalem. "All three parties made mistakes, and in such complex negotiations, everyone is bound to. But no one is solely to blame."

This analysis suggests that a breakdown was not as inevitable as it now appears. It shows how the leaders were often driven by public-opinion polls at home to take positions that made achieving a peace more difficult, and then often misjudged how the other side would react. The analysis also reveals how the story that emerged, blaming Arafat and the Palestinians, helped harden positions in Israel against continuing negotiations, thus further dimming hopes for peace.

Yet these same diplomats and experts say that neither side can win the current struggle. Eventually, both will have to come back to peace talks and base them on the rough outlines that were under discussion in 2000.

How close were the two sides to peace? Days before the peace process was severely damaged by Palestinian riots in September 2000, Barak and Arafat held an unusually congenial dinner meeting in Barak's private residence. At one point during the dinner, Barak even called President Clinton and excitedly told the President that he and Arafat were going to strike a peace bargain. Within earshot of the Palestinian leader, Barak theatrically announced, "I'm going to be the partner of this man."

Unintended Consequences

But the dinner was also a classic example of how misunderstandings and communication failures can lead to unintended consequences.

Arafat says that during the dinner, he huddled with Barak on the balcony, imploring him to block a planned visit by Ariel Sharon, then leader of Israel's major opposition party, to the Temple Mount in Jerusalem, a place of tremendous religious significance.

To Jews, the Temple Mount is sacred as the site of the temple of Herod the Great, of which only a supporting wall, the Western Wall, remains. Muslims revere the site as al-Haram al-Sharif (Holy Sanctuary), where Muhammad is believed to have ascended into heaven.

Arafat felt that Sharon's visit would be a provocation. But Barak's government did not act to prevent the visit, perceiving it as an internal Israeli political matter involving Sharon's jockeying for power against a rival in his party.

That was a major miscalculation. Sharon's visit under heavy guard, intended to demonstrate Israeli sovereignty over the Temple Mount, set off angry Palestinian demonstrations. The Israelis used lethal force to put them down. The cycle of violence started.

Playing upon Israeli fears of violence and arguing that the Palestinians weren't interested in peace, Sharon ran for Prime Minister against Barak and won in February 2001.

Since then, the U.S. has continued efforts to bring the two sides together, although President George W. Bush says his administration will be less active than Clinton's was in the peace effort. In spring 2001, former U.S. Senator George Mitchell mapped out a plan for both sides to re-enter peace negotiations. In June 2001, CIA Director George Tenet managed to negotiate a cease-fire, based on Mitchell's recommendations. The agreement briefly reduced violence, then fell apart. By late August 2001, new negotiations to restore the cease-fire had been planned, and a return to the peace table seemed possible.

Creating a Final Peace

The Camp David talks in the summer of 2000 were intended to hammer out a final peace agreement, after seven years of negotiating between the two sides that had begun in Oslo, Norway, in 1993. The goal was to solve problems left over from the Six-Day War of 1967, when Israel attacked its Arab neighbors and captured the Sinai Peninsula, the Golan Heights, the Gaza Strip, and the West Bank, home of 1.5 million Palestinians.

The core issues of the current struggle: Palestinians insist that Israel must turn over sufficient land in the West Bank and Gaza Strip to allow the creation of a Palestinian state. Some Israelis fear that such a state in their midst could threaten Israel's security or even lead to its destruction.

Over the years, the conflict has sprouted layer upon layer of complexity. [In the summer of 2000], negotiators argued endlessly over how much territory in the West Bank would be given to Palestinians, over the division of Jerusalem (claimed by Israel as its capital and by the Palestinians as the capital of their would-be nation), over whether Palestinian refugees would be allowed to return to the homes they fled during the wars, over the future of Jewish settlements built through the years in territory the Palestinians claim as their own, and over what security measures could protect Israel from violence.

High Hopes, Broken Trust

As the Camp David talks began, there was extraordinary optimism that they would produce a historic agreement. But it now seems clear that Palestinians came to the talks feeling pressured by Barak, who needed a peace deal to bolster his re-election hopes, and by Clinton who, in the waning days of his presidency, hoped that a Mideast peace would brighten his legacy.

The Palestinians said too that the Americans did not seem to take seriously the pressures of the Palestinian public and the Muslim world on Arafat. Like Barak, Arafat went to Camp David dogged by plummeting domestic approval ratings.

In addition, there was the background to the talks: mutual distrust that seven years of peace talks had not undone. Right-wing Israeli politicians complained that the Palestinian leadership was not educating its people for peace, not collecting illegal weapons, and not acting to reduce incitement against Israel.

The Palestinians, for their part, lost faith in Israeli promises to transfer land to them as the dates for doing so were routinely delayed and Jewish settlements were expanded in territory the Palestinians believe to be theirs.

How poorly did things go between Barak and Arafat at Camp David? According to a Palestinian observer, during one dinner, with Clinton sitting between the two leaders, Barak spent the evening ignoring Arafat and talking with Clinton's daughter, Chelsea.

But critics also point out that the Palestinians failed to come up with counterproposals to what the Israelis were offering. Bob Malley, Clinton's chief Mideast adviser at Camp David, wrote in *The New York Times* in mid-July 2001 that the Palestinian passivity frustrated American mediators "almost to the point of despair."

Setting the Clock Back?

Despite the problems, however, progress was made at Camp David. The Israelis offered concessions on turning over territory in Jerusalem that they had never made before. And the Palestinians, in turn, assented to Israeli rule over key Jewish neighborhoods and religious sites, and agreed to accept several Jewish settlements they had opposed for years.

But in the aftermath of Camp David, critics say Clinton made a blunder, praising Barak and saying Arafat had not made an equivalent effort.

"Clinton left us to our own devices after he started the blame game," says Shlomo Ben-Ami, Israel's Foreign Minister at the time. "He was trying to give Barak a boost, knowing he had political problems going home empty-handed. But in doing so, he created problems with the other side."

Yet peace negotiations did not die then, or even in September 2000 when the Palestinian riots broke out following Sharon's visit to the Temple Mount. In fact, few Israelis, Palestinians, or Americans realize how much diplomatic activity continued after the Camp David meeting. All the negotiating came to a head in January 2001 in Taba, Egypt, where Israeli and Palestinian negotiators met again, with an American peace plan on the table. Unknown to anyone in the public, those negotiations came as close to achieving peace as any diplomatic effort has done in more than 30 years.

But time ran out. Although much progress had been made, the negotiations were finally suspended by Israel because elections were imminent. In short order, Clinton left office, and Barak lost his position as Prime Minister to Sharon. Amid mounting violence, some Israelis and Palestinians have come to believe that the clock has been set back decades.

Distrust on both sides has skyrocketed, with many Israelis now believing that Arafat has been completely discredited as a "peace partner." At the same time, many Palestinians fear that far-right parties in Sharon's coalition government will push the extremist view that Palestinians should be "transferred" to neighboring Arab lands.

Yet relatively few Israelis, Palestinians, or outside observers believe that there can be a military solution to the conflict. Thus, the two sides will eventually have to return to serious talks.

And in fact, those who played key roles in the negotiations still believe a peace built on the near miss in 2000 is possible.

"Clinton took us on a futuristic voyage," says Saeb Erekat, a senior Palestinian negotiator. "We have seen the endgame. It's just a matter of time."

Says Gilad Sher, a senior Israeli negotiator: "I still think that peace is doable, feasible, and reasonable. That's the tragedy, because the basis of the agreement is lying there, in arm's reach."

CHAPTER 2

ARAB AND ISRAELI
APPROACHES TO THE
CONFLICT

Contemporary Issues
Companion

THE CYCLE OF VIOLENCE: AN OVERVIEW

Serge Schmemann

In the late 1990s, it appeared as if there was finally going to be peace in Israel, reports Serge Schmemann in the following selection. However, in October 2000, a new outbreak of violence began after Ariel Sharon, then a member of Israel's parliament, made a highly public and controversial visit to a contested holy site, accompanied by a large contingent of armed guards. Schmemann explains that several Palestinians protesting Sharon's action were killed by Israeli security forces, which in turn led to violent retaliation by Palestinians and further crackdowns by the Israeli military. According to Schmemann, this cycle of violence is typical of the history of the Arab-Israeli conflict: Both sides believe that the other only understands the use of force. As long as the leaders of both the Israelis and the Palestinians see the use of force as their only option, Schmemann observes, peace in Israel will remain out of reach. Schmemann is the deputy foreign editor for the *New York Times.*

Ariel Sharon was 14 when he joined the underground Jewish army, and he fought in the Arab-Israeli war that started the day after the creation of the Jewish state. Yasir Arafat was smuggling arms to Palestinians by 17, in an attempt to destroy the new nation that displaced so many of his people.

Enemies from the beginning, Sharon and Arafat—now the leaders of Israel and the Palestinians—in many ways represent the history of their respective struggles, and the reasons why it has been so difficult for the two sides to make peace and share the land where they live.

Some experts believe the two sides could already be drawing a border between Israel and a separate state of Palestine in a way that would be fair to both. The problem is how to get there through the deep-rooted ambitions, distrust, and grievances both sides hold.

In 2000, the Israelis and Palestinians came closer than they had ever been to making peace—only to descend into the worst bloodshed

Serge Schmemann, "Face-Off," *New York Times Upfront,* vol. 134, May 6, 2002, p. 16. Copyright © 2002 by The New York Times Company and Scholastic Inc. Reproduced by permission.

in their long and complicated history. The fighting became especially brutal in March and April 2002, when Sharon, infuriated by Palestinian suicide bombings that were killing many Israelis, ordered tanks and soldiers to invade Palestinian cities and towns, to uproot the "infrastructure of terrorism." But the civilian cost was enormous in lives, property, and anguish.

The current crisis is a sharp contrast to the hopes raised in 1993, when Yitzhak Rabin, then Prime Minister of Israel, signed a historic land-for-peace deal with Arafat. Under the agreement, which came to be known as the Oslo accords, for the Norwegian city where they were negotiated, Israel accepted in principle the creation of a Palestinian state in return for Palestinian recognition of the state of Israel, and a pledge by Arafat to stop violent action against it.

The agreement laid out a process of several stages, starting with Palestinian self-rule in major towns and villages, and ending with a full peace settlement. But a Jewish extremist assassinated Rabin in 1995. Under the subsequent government, the Oslo process became mired in bickering and outbreaks of violence until 1999, when Israelis elected Ehud Barak, a close associate of Rabin, as Prime Minister.

In August 2000, President Bill Clinton brought Barak and Arafat to Camp David, in the mountains of Maryland, to revive the talks. Barak offered concessions on key issues—the borders between Israel and the proposed nation of Palestine, the division of Jerusalem (claimed by both sides as their capital), and the fate of Palestinian refugees who seek to return to their former homes in Israel. Arafat turned them down.

A Setback to Peace

A month later, Sharon, then a member of Israel's parliament, made a provocative visit to a sacred site in Jerusalem known to Jews as the Temple Mount, and to Muslims as Haram al-Sharif (Noble Sanctuary). The base of the plateau is Judaism's holiest site of worship, the remains of Solomon's Temple. The summit of the mount is the third-holiest site in Islam, revered as the place from which the Prophet Muhammad dreamed of ascending to heaven.

Sharon entered the walled-in summit with 1,000 security guards, enraging the Palestinians. Reports at the time said the visit was intended to build Sharon's standing among conservative Israelis. But he could have had no doubt that it would generate fierce and probably violent protests, setting back continuing efforts to negotiate a peace settlement.

Several Palestinian protesters were killed in clashes with Israeli security forces, prompting further protests in the West Bank and Gaza Strip. As the fighting escalated, many Israelis came to believe that Arafat, having rejected the Camp David offers, now wanted to use increasing street violence to put new pressure on Israel. Israelis reacted by voting overwhelmingly in 2001 to elect the hawkish, conservative Sharon as their Prime Minister.

The Israelis turned to Sharon because he had a reputation as a tough, uncompromising general and politician. He had condemned the Oslo accords as dangerous, and had never ceased regarding Arafat and the Palestine Liberation Organization (PLO) as terrorists.

Two Very Different Leaders

Sharon is a member of the generation of Israelis who fought for much of their lives for the very existence of Israel. Born in Palestine in 1928, he took part in all of Israel's wars, developing a reputation for ruthlessness. In 1982, as defense minister, Sharon ordered an invasion of Lebanon in an attempt to drive out Palestinian guerrillas. During that campaign, hundreds of Palestinians were massacred by Lebanese militiamen in two refugee camps. An Israeli investigation later held Sharon indirectly responsible for the killings.

As a leader in subsequent Israeli governments, Sharon was instrumental in building Jewish settlements on Israeli-occupied Arab lands. These settlements became a central source of Palestinian grievances against Israel. So when Sharon came to office, there was little doubt of his attitude toward Arafat and the Palestinians.

Arafat is also a veteran and a survivor. Born in 1929, probably in Cairo, he spent his university years in political activities. He helped found Al Fatah, an underground guerrilla network, which eventually became the largest group in the PLO. Year after year, the PLO launched bloody attacks against Israel, and Arafat gained a reputation as a ruthless terrorist.

As head of the PLO, Arafat became the leader of the Palestinian national movement and a symbol of the Palestinian struggle. In 1996, Arafat was overwhelmingly elected chairman of the Palestinian Authority, which administers Palestinian-controlled portions of the Gaza Strip and the West Bank.

Old Enemies Reverting to Old Ways

With the resumption in fighting, each man reverted to his old ways. Sharon made no secret of his hatred, declaring Arafat an "enemy," blaming him for all the terror attacks against Israel, and sealing him up for weeks in his Ramallah office. Arafat became the guerrilla, allowing militant groups to launch devastating suicide bombings against Israel, and posing proudly in his darkened office with an automatic pistol.

Although most Israelis and Palestinians would insist they want peace, the mutual distrust and hatred is so high, and the grievances so many, that neither side seems capable of breaking the cycle of violence. Many Israelis fear that the Palestinians will never stop attacking them, and that only force can protect them. And the Palestinians, after the vicious attacks on their territory, are determined to continue their uprising, believing that only violence brings them closer to their goal of ending the Israeli occupation and establishing a Palestinian state.

But both Israelis and Palestinians have broken out of the cycle before, when Prime Minister Rabin shook hands with Arafat in 1993. At some point, the two sides may again realize that they cannot achieve their ends through force and finally find a way to coexist. And if Sharon and Arafat are still in charge, they may finally cap their careers as warriors and politicians with the wreath of victors.

TERROR TACTICS ARE OFFICIAL PALESTINIAN POLICY

Martin Peretz

In the following selection, Martin Peretz maintains that the use of terrorist tactics such as suicide bombings is a routine policy of Palestinian leader Yasser Arafat and the Palestine Liberation Organization. This policy was put in place even before the Israelis began their occupation of the West Bank and the Gaza Strip in 1967, he argues, and the use of this strategy has only accelerated since then. Palestinians have been offered peace time and again, the author contends, but they will not be satisfied until they have taken over all of Israel. Peretz believes that Arafat and the Palestinians desire nothing less than an all-out war against Jews—a fact the international community has yet to acknowledge. Instead, he asserts, many world leaders condemn Israel for taking steps to defend itself against terrorist attacks. Peretz is the editor in chief of the *New Republic*, a weekly news journal.

I don't remember when I first heard this Yiddish verse, written by an unknown poet in the Warsaw Ghetto. But I know I was then still a child, and its cadences have haunted me ever since:

> *In the Warsaw Ghetto it is the month of spring.*
> *And full on the table stands Elijah's cup.*
> *But who, to this seder, does ruin bring?*
> *The Angel of Death, who comes to drink and sup.*

We were preparing our Passover seder [in March 2002] at the New York apartment of one of our children when we heard the grim news that the angel of death had intruded on another seder, this time a communal one in Netanya, Israel, reaping a harvest of 25 dead. This macabre angel remained especially active in the days that followed; and one week later, the number of Israeli noncombatants dead in other suicide killings had risen to 45, with the toll of the disfigured and injured climbing into the hundreds.

Theodor Herzl wrote that Zionism's twin goals were to allow the Jewish people to "live at last as free men on our own soil, and in our homes peacefully die." And Zionism has achieved the first: a democratic, modern, liberal society, curious, scientific, on the cutting edge of medicine, accountable, transparent, and extremely plural. (Whatever hardships Arab citizens of Israel endure, they are mostly attributable to the unremitting enmity to Israel of their cousins in the neighborhood; and they are, still, the freest Arabs in the region.) Still, the second goal remains elusive. The Jews of Israel still cannot be sure that they will be allowed to die peacefully in their homes. In fact, the angel of death has intruded on their ordinary civilian lives for more than one century now.

The killings of Jews by Palestinians—and, earlier, by Arabs who didn't yet consider themselves Palestinians—predated the establishment of the state of Israel. The killers did not differentiate among their targets. They just had to be Jews, random Jews, any Jews: socialist farmers on some remote kibbutz in the Galilee, working people in Haifa, or ultrapious (and, for that matter, often anti-Zionist) men and women from a town like Hebron where Jews had lived innocuously and continuously since several centuries before Mohammed set foot on this earth.

Nor, for that matter, is the specific phenomenon of suicidal murder altogether an innovation of contemporary Arab and Muslim fanatics. This has been a hot subject in historic Islam for centuries, and it remains so in the mosques and schools of higher Muslim learning today, pro and con. The widespread adulation of Al Qaeda and the Al Aqsa Martyrs Brigade, of Osama bin Laden and Yasir Arafat, of Mohammed Atta and the young man on his way to paradise because he perpetrated mass murder in Tel Aviv, is evidence of the deep roots that this practice has in the culture of the Arab and Muslim world. And let us name the phenomenon honestly. When pampered Saudi princes praise the "martyrs of Palestine," and when Arafat himself says (more than a bit insincerely) that he wishes to die a shahid, they are (as Shimon Peres has pointed out) countenancing the idea of human sacrifice as an active agent of modern politics.

Terror Attacks Predate the Occupation

It is particularly disturbing that Pope John Paul II seems not to have grasped this. And, in his Easter 2002 message "to the City and to the World," during which he enunciated that tired cliche that "no one can remain silent" about Israeli aggression, he found it quite easy to be silent about the Palestinians' now-habitual dependence on human sacrifice as tactic and strategy. Of course, Arafat is an old pal of the pontiff, having visited the Vatican almost as frequently as he visited Bill Clinton's White House. And there is a deep cynicism to the pope's moral equivalence between the premeditated murder admired and practiced by literally every flank and faction in the Palestinian polity and the unintended victims of Israel's rather scrupulous and, indeed, finicky war against terror (up to the recent days, mostly the bombing of empty buildings.)

Yasir Arafat, of course, has never been finicky about terrorism, and his long history on that score mocks America's calls for him to renounce the only craft he has ever truly known. Arafat's debut on the world stage coincides with the beginning of the Palestinian revolution, which, it is urgent to recall, commenced at least three years before the Six Day War. This means that Arafat started the Palestine Liberation Organization before one Israeli ever stepped foot into the West Bank or Gaza Strip—or, for that matter, prayed at the Western Wall in Jerusalem or walked in the city's ancient Jewish Quarter. There were no "occupied territories" back then, and there weren't really any disputed territories either—except in the heads of the Palestinians. What Arafat wanted then (and what I believe he still wants now) was to liberate not Hebron or Nablus or Gaza (which in 1967 were in Arab hands) but Haifa and Tel Aviv, the plains of Sharon, and the Negev desert. Or, as military historian Victor Davis Hanson put it in *The Wall Street Journal*, "the current Arab-Israeli war—at least the fourth fought since 1948—is fought over the West Bank: but that is only because . . . the Arab world lost the first three wars to destroy Israel proper."

From the beginning, Arafat's tactics of terror were audacious: blowing up airplanes in midair; taking children hostage in schoolhouses; skyjackings; hijacking of buses; shootouts and bombings in crowded airports, theaters, terminals, markets, beaches, restaurants, wedding halls. His most daring moment was during the 1972 Munich Olympics, in which eleven Israeli athletes lost their lives. (It was also the first moment when Peter Jennings showed himself to be oh, so understanding of Palestinian terror.) But this terrorism occurred only sporadically. It wasn't until the Oslo agreements and the handshake on the White House lawn that Arafat's terrorism became a routine feature of life in Israel. Israel obliged itself in 1993 to provide the Palestinian Authority weapons (augmented, of course, by the armaments the Palestinians smuggled and illegally manufactured themselves). And those weapons became the instruments of Jewish death. The closer the Israelis came to meeting Palestinian demands, the more intense the terror became. Suicide bombing, in fact, didn't become the Palestinians' chosen mode of day in, day out terror until the year 2000, when Israel offered Arafat more than the old butcher probably ever expected.

Even my friend Tom Friedman, generally much too credulous about Arafat's intentions, recently wrote that the Palestinian president and his compatriots "have not chosen suicide bombing out of 'desperation.'" The Palestinians, he says, were offered "a peace plan that could have ended their 'desperate' occupation, and Yasir Arafat walked away." He goes on to say that the Palestinians "want to win their independence in blood and fire," and that is because "all they can agree on is what they want to destroy not what they want to build. . . . Let's be very clear: Palestinians have adopted suicide bombing as a strategic choice. . . . This threatens all civilization because if suicide bombing is allowed to work in Israel, then, like hijacking and airplane bombing, it will be copied and will eventually lead to a bomber strapped with a nuclear device threatening entire nations."

Arafat's International Allies

If Friedman is right—and I believe he is—then the solicitude for Arafat expressed by so many world leaders is itself perilous. Prince Sultan, the Saudi defense minister, called the siege of Ramallah "the greatest crime in the history of humanity." Is he out of his head? The Lebanese president's bleatings on Arafat's behalf are more than a little hypocritical given his decision to prevent Arafat's speech from Ramallah from being heard live at the Beirut summit. As for the threat by Jordan's foreign minister, Marwan Muasher, to send the Israeli ambassador back to Jerusalem, he is playing an old, and silly, game. The Hashemites know all too well that Israeli intelligence is their first line of defense against their menacing Arab neighbors and that the Israeli military is their second. That has been clear since at least 1970, when the Israelis turned back Syrian tank divisions heading toward Amman. Israel guarantees Jordan's survival. The king and his Cabinet can express their "deep anger" at Israel's treatment of Arafat; but, in truth, he is a threat to them as well, and as such they wish him nothing but ill. King Abdullah and his advisers surely don't want Israel to give Arafat all the territories captured from them in 1967, and they were desolated when it seemed that Ehud Barak would do just that. They want the Jordan Valley in Jewish hands—as a buffer between emergent Palestine and their own country and also to prevent chaos among the West Bank Palestinians from spreading to the Palestinians in their own kingdom.

Arafat's most sincere partisans are not in the Arab world; they are in the nations of Europe, whose leaders routinely threaten Israel with retribution when it seeks to defend itself. Some of this is domestic politics: European leaders must now cater to ever larger, and more militant, Arab and Muslim populations within their own borders (a fact that should give pause to Americans who wish to indiscriminately admit immigrants who would bring their old hatreds to their new home). In the diplomatic strutting of European states that once deployed real force around the world but now no longer can, there is probably also some nostalgia for empire. Who really cares, after all, what Belgium thinks about Israel's conflict with the Arabs? The European states and, for that matter, U.N. Secretary-General Kofi Annan are structurally incapable of truly influencing events on the ground in Israel, the disputed territories, or the rest of the Arab world. They cannot produce a real concession from Israel because they cannot produce—and haven't—even a symbolic concession from the Palestinians. And, for all their patronage and nurturing of Arafat, he has never given them even a diplomatic crumb to take to Israel.

The European country that has hectored Israel the longest and most obsessively, of course, is France. And why should we be surprised? After all, President Jacques Chirac and Prime Minister Lionel Jospin's attacks on the Jewish state have accompanied a frightening intensification of anti-Semitism in France.

A War Against Jews

Then there is the left—like the people who went to be with Arafat inside his compound [in April 2002]. These "progressives" are not a new phenomenon in world affairs: They and their ancestors have been worshiping bloodthirsty leaders for more than half a century. But with Stalin, Mao, and Castro, there was, for a time, at least a veneer of brutal idealism. Zionism was an expression of European liberalism, and there were Arab intellectuals who imagined that their nationalism also would be nurtured by that source. But, in practice, Arab nationalism has become a very nasty business, defined everywhere by dictatorship. Palestinian nationalism is no different. Arafat has no grand vision of human affairs whatsoever, no desire other than territory—and territory not as the seedbed for an inspired vision of community but as a launching pad for war against the Jews.

Arafat could not possibly have stirred these activists' dreams of a just society, because he has none. His scant program contains not even the deceit of egalitarianism. Arafat is a fascist, and his fascism has at its very core the hatred of Jews. And since he is unabashedly stirred by this passion, one has to suspect his admirers as well, all of them. . . . In France, already, synagogues are being burned and cemeteries trashed. And in Israel, amidst a rage of daily terror, a young Palestinian came to the seder door and murdered 25 men and women, one pregnant with two children in her belly, never to see the light of day.

PALESTINIANS RESORT TO TERROR TACTICS OUT OF DESPAIR

Eyad El Sarraj, interviewed by Linda Butler

Psychiatrist Eyad El Sarraj is the founder and director of the Gaza Community Mental Health Programme, which provides mental health services to the residents of the Gaza Strip. In the following selection, he discusses Palestinian terror tactics with Linda Butler, the associate editor of the *Journal of Palestine Studies*. According to El Sarraj, the harsh realities of living under Israeli occupation cause many Palestinians to sink into hopelessness and despair. Feeling that they have little to live for, and trusting in the belief that martyrs will be rewarded in the afterlife, some Palestinians choose to become suicide bombers, he asserts. Furthermore, El Sarraj maintains, Palestinians do not possess the same degree of military strength as the Israeli government, so many feel that terrorist tactics are the only effective weapons they have against the Israelis. While El Sarraj stresses that he personally does not agree with the use of such tactics, he insists that it is essential to understand the mindset that leads oppressed Palestinians to become martyrs for their cause.

Linda Butler: At the time of Oslo, many people commented on how Palestinians were willing to "forgive and forget" the occupation and put the past behind them. Today, in the light of what has happened, especially in the West Bank, will this be so easy?

Eyad El Sarraj: Of course the distrust and hatred are far deeper now. One of [Israeli prime minister Ariel] Sharon's great victories is the way he has increased the level of hatred on both sides. If the strategy was to destroy any possibility of peace, he has scored a huge success.

Still, if there is a solution that is fair—and I mean the 1967 borders, a shared Jerusalem, a fair resolution for the refugees, dismantled settlements—I believe the Palestinians will accept it, and the Israelis too. If that happened, it would change dramatically the psychology of the people on both sides. But if the Palestinians come out feeling that

Linda Butler, "Suicide Bombers: Dignity, Despair, and the Need for Hope: An Interview with Eyad El Sarraj," *Journal of Palestine Studies*, vol. 31, Summer 2002, p. 71. Copyright © 2002 by University of California Press. Reproduced by permission of the publisher.

they have been defeated, the solution won't last. There will be new violence, and even greater violence, the way each cycle is more violent than what preceded.

In that regard, can you compare the two intifadas?

Let me tell you first that the people who are committing the suicide bombings in this intifada are the children of the first intifada—people who witnessed so much trauma as children. So as they grew up, their own identity merged with the national identity of humiliation and defeat, and they avenge that defeat at both the personal and national levels. That is one observation.

The escalation of the level of violence is unbelievable. In the first intifada it was stones at best. In this intifada it's machine guns and homemade mortars and explosives and especially suicide bombings. The next intifada, which, if there is no solution, will certainly happen in another four to seven years, will be even worse than we have witnessed in the last two years.

Psychological Factors

Aside from weapons, to what do you attribute this extraordinary escalation of violence in the second intifada? Is there a psychological dimension as well?

Of course. It's despair. The hopelessness that comes from a situation that keeps getting worse, a despair where living becomes no different from dying. Desperation is a very powerful force—it's not only negative. It propels people to actions or solutions that previously would have been unthinkable. What is unthinkable today becomes accepted tomorrow. Whoever would have imagined suicide bombings in Palestine ten years ago? There is no precedent in our society. This is what I mean when I say that if this continues, there will be new methods of escalation of the violence too horrific even to imagine today.

Listen. In the last uprising, children used to play a game called "intifada." It was a cowboys-and-Indians-type game—more specifically, Israeli soldier versus Palestinian stone thrower, with the kids trading off between the role of the soldiers armed with sticks to represent guns and the Palestinians with kufiyyahs [a type of headdress] and stones. Many of the children at the time preferred to play the Jew, basically because the Jew with the guns represented power. This game has entirely disappeared. Today, the symbol of power is the martyr. If you ask a child in Gaza today what he wants to be when he grows up, he doesn't say that he wants to be a doctor or a soldier or an engineer. He says he wants to be a martyr.

How has this happened, from identifying with power, even of the oppressor, to wanting to die?

People, including young people, need to feel respected. They want status within their society. Today the martyr is glorified. The martyr for them is the power of the people, the power to take revenge on behalf of the victims. They have all these romantic notions. They see the martyr as courageously sacrificing himself or herself for the sake of everyone, as a symbol of the struggle for freedom, because this is what these people are fighting for.

So all these are different meanings of power, especially in light of the demolition of the father image in the eyes of the children. During the first intifada, studies showed that 55 percent of the children had witnessed their fathers being humiliated or beaten by Israeli soldiers. The psychological impact of this is stunning. The father, normally the authority figure, comes to be seen as somebody who is helpless, who can't even protect himself—let alone his children. So children became more militant, more violent. People are the products of their environment. Children who have seen so much inhumanity—basically the Israeli occupation policies—inevitably come out with inhuman responses. That's really how to understand the suicide bombings.

Becoming Suicide Bombers

Of course, in the last analysis, the suicide bombings have given the Israelis an excuse to come in. This being the case, is there a popular reaction against suicide bombings as a factor contributing to their suffering?

Well, you see, suicide bombings and all these forms of violence— I'm talking as a doctor here—are only the symptoms, the reaction to this chronic and systematic process of humiliating people in effort to destroy their hope and dignity. That is the illness, and unless it is resolved and treated, there will be more and more symptoms of the pathology.

Before I left Gaza this time, one of our child psychiatrists at the clinic told me how some of the children he is treating tell him about how they are passing their time—not with games, but trying to manufacture mortar—figuring out how they can do it by hand. One can imagine that some of them might start thinking of chemical weapons or projectile suicide bombings.

You talk about suicide bombings being, in a way, a psychological response to the occupation, but to what extent are they manipulated by Hamas and other such groups?

Hamas has its own ideology. I'm not really versed in this, but as far as I know, they have an ideology that calls for an Islamic state in all of Palestine through holy war and killing the enemy. They believe that the Israelis can only listen to the language of force. To that end, they are ready to use any means, including suicide bombings. And there are plenty of volunteers. . . .

Palestinians Do Not Teach Hatred

But do they encourage these children to volunteer? When the Holy Land Foundation, the leading Muslim charity in the United States, was closed by President [George W.] Bush after 11 September, one of the reasons cited was that the organization funded charities supported by Hamas, reported to extol suicide bombings in the schools and through active recruitment. . . .

This is false, of course. Americans also talk about the way the Palestinian curriculum in general promotes hatred against Jews. But if you look at both curricula, you'll see that there is nothing that teaches this hatred. You don't need schools for that—all you need is to see Israeli soldiers humiliating your father or Phantom-16s destroying your homes, and the message gets through. Hamas doesn't need to recruit. One of my colleagues told me about a patient who became very depressed when he was passed over as a suicide bomber; he had missed his chance to be a martryr.

Maybe this is difficult to understand in the West, though in the West, too, you glorify your war dead, you build memorials to those who fall for the nation. In every society, such people are respected. But to this you have to add the level of utter despair that's in the territories, the hopelessness. And added to this is the religious notion that life begins with death. This is what religious people believe. The militant ones believe that if they die as suicide fighters in the struggle for justice, they are conquering defeat and death itself—that they don't die, that with death they begin to live (though this talk of the virgins in Paradise is rubbish, and no one has done it for that). If life is intolerable, with no hope, and if there's a promise that if you die as a martyr you'll have a new and better life, why not take the chance?

Of course, in Islam, suicide for personal reasons is a sin; it's forbidden. But martyrdom is something else. And there are so many interpretations of suicide bombing, because obviously, it didn't exist at the time of the Prophet Muhammad—in fact, it's an entirely new phenomenon in Islam. It was first practiced by Hizballah after Israel occupied southern Lebanon in 1982, and the highest Egyptian and Saudi religious authorities have ruled against it. So it is very much debated in Islam: Is it a form of sacrificing yourself for God? Is it acceptable to kill civilians? The militant Muslims say that all Israelis are military people anyway, including women. Another argument, even by Hamas, is that they wouldn't turn their bodies into bombs if they had F-16s, Apache helicopters, tanks, or a tiny fraction of the weapons Israel gets from the United States. They say that if you want to attack an Israeli soldier—who is absolutely invulnerable in his bunker or tank—how else can you do it? To their minds, the Israelis have the power of the F-16s, while we have the power to die. So we have reached this deeply paranoid position.

I personally am totally against suicide bombings, on principle, on moral grounds. I believe that Islam is about life. Islam tells us that we must protect women and children and even trees during war. These are the words of the Prophet Muhammad. So under Islam, how can you kill yourself and innocent civilians in this way? But militant Muslims have different interpretations.

Celebrating Death

From press reports here, one often gets the impression of a kind of celebra-
tory atmosphere within families whose sons were killed as suicide bombers,
which reinforces the notion that, in contrast to Israelis, Palestinians don't
care very much about human life or even their own flesh and blood. There is
also talk of financial reward, that the families get money.

Anyone who actually believes such an interpretation is in a process
of racist dehumanization. How can you believe in your own humanity if you don't believe in the humanity of the enemy?

But about this atmosphere of celebration you mention, this is the
way our culture reacts to death under any circumstances. In our tradition, when someone dies people go to the families for days on end to
pay their respects. The customary formulas are that this man or
woman has been blessed, has been called by God, so that we should
not be sad but should actually be happy for this person who is now
with God. Everyone says these things to the family to help them get
through their feelings of loss and grief. And this continues for forty
days, this support—this is the tradition.

Now when it comes to a person who has sacrificed himself or herself for God, they are even more respected. They reach a status of holi-
ness in the eyes of the people for reasons I already described. And the
overwhelming support of society helps the family deal with the loss.
There's the heroism of dying for others, of not accepting humiliation
and defeat, and more than that, of being supported by God, and that
whatever happens to us is a test of our faith. We have to be good Muslims to please God. And the ultimate way to be a good Muslim, they
think, is to die for God.

So this is the atmosphere. Later on, of course, the families begin to
feel it, in what we call delayed grief reaction. Once all this social support and solidarity subsides and they're left on their own, they start to
realize: Where is my son? And they feel the pain like anyone else.

As for the money, of course people support the martyrs' families. I
myself am deeply opposed to suicide bombings, yet I too support the
families. As a Palestinian, as an Arab, as a Muslim, and as a human
being, I feel obliged to support them. I cannot leave their children in
poverty—I have to do what I can to leave them some hope and dignity. This is why we support the families—certainly not to encourage
suicide bombing. And no person has ever become a martyr for such
reasons.

Terrorism Is Damaging Palestinian Society

One hears that there's a debate in Palestinian society about the militariza-
tion of the second intifada and especially the suicide phenomenon, that
there are those who think that this has been very damaging.

There is a debate among the intellectuals, but among the people,
it's not there yet—not in this atmosphere, when people are under

siege, under attack. There's a deep anger, defiance, so even if people know deep down that these tactics will not bring a solution, they still support them. It's an emotional reaction.

In Palestinian political circles, there is a debate. It's not about morality; it's about politics: Is anything achieved from suicide bombing or not? And I believe that more and more people are beginning to realize that it's completely counterproductive, disastrous, and that politically all it does is radicalize Israelis, who continue to support Sharon—who feeds off this—and give him justification to do whatever he wants. More and more people believe this, but so far it's especially in intellectual circles.

Have there been studies about the long-term effects of this kind of violence on a society, for example in Bosnia?

I haven't seen any studies about Bosnia, but all you have to do is look at places where there was a particularly brutal colonial regime and see what happened later. The violence among the South African black townships after independence. And Algeria, where the level of brutality and atrocity the French exercised was almost unimaginable—mass murder, whole villages wiped out, and so on. They were determined to totally obliterate the Algerian culture. All this was taken into the psyche of the Algerian people, and today you have this suppressed rage being turned against themselves.

This doesn't bode well. . . .

All it means is that there is an absolute need for a thorough and deep process of national reconciliation that allows Palestinians to come to terms with their pain, their trauma, their grief and loss—and the same thing for the Israelis, by the way. But it can't happen without a political solution first, one that is fair and dignified and gives hope.

So what does this mean for the Palestinian society, long run? People have been writing for some time about an upsurge in violence in Gaza over the years, even of a certain disintegration of society. . . .

There is no question that violence has increased, but you have to realize that it's starting from a very low threshold: If you knew Gaza before 1967, homicide was practically unheard of—maybe one every few years. But over the years, with the violence of the occupation and the violence it brought to the society, it has increased—political violence, violence against women, and so on. But it should be mentioned that the violence is restricted to the political level or within the social network. Violence is within the family, within the tribe, or along tribal lines. If you are an ordinary person who isn't involved in politics or clan feuds, you're absolutely safe. There's no anonymous or random or chaotic violence here. That hasn't changed.

And you can't say society is disintegrating in that the tribal or clan structure is still very much intact. This is the structure people rely on for security and for protection, for support and help.

Palestinians Will Endure

Do you see it as a source of hope, in a way?

No, it is not a source of hope; it's a source of endurance. Once there is peace, it's something we have to move beyond and learn true notions of citizenship. But in times of siege, under extreme duress, it enables people to live, to survive. This is the history of Gaza, where the state has always been alien. This is the way people lived for centuries, relying on themselves and their clan. It's part of the reason for the extraordinary resilience of people. Gaza has not been under siege like the West Bank, but even here, you can't move around, you're under closure, the power is cut, water is scarce. You can't get to hospitals. And yet people manage; they make do. Under the heavy cloud of despair and frustration and helplessness, there is still deep conviction and very strong feeling of defiance, coupled with the feeling that God is with us—that He is testing us now, but that He will come to our aid. All this means that people can still endure, and it ensures that with new layers of confrontation, if it continues, the people will still be there.

These people can take so much, I tell you. They can take so much more, so much more. That's why, deep inside, they are still so defiant.

Do you see hope in the long term?

Yes, absolutely. I believe in the basic humanity of our people. And I believe that there will be peace, because there's no other option. More and more people will see that killing and murder are not the solution. Even Israeli military experts, like [Benjamin] Ben-Eliezer, say there is no military solution. More and more people will come to this. What I hope is that this happens sooner rather than later so that we can spare the lives of so many people who don't need to die—this is what I hope. It's possible that there will be a few more thousand on each side, but if, at the end of the day, we're going to reach a peaceful solution based on what we already know, why should there be all these deaths?

Israel's Response to Palestinian Terrorism Is Justified

Facts and Logic About the Middle East

Facts and Logic About the Middle East (FLAME) is an organization that is dedicated to publishing information about the Arab-Israeli conflict through letters to editors and paid advertisements. The following selection addresses Israel's response to violent Palestinian uprisings in the occupied territories. FLAME contends that Israel is only doing what it has to do in order to maintain law and order. Members of the Israeli Defense Force (IDF) are confronted daily by violent riots and deadly, unpredictable attacks, FLAME asserts. Nevertheless, the IDF responds with as much restraint as possible in quelling these incidents, according to the authors, and only uses deadly force when absolutely necessary. It is unfortunate that some Arabs lose their lives in these confrontations, but Israel is obligated to protect itself and its people, the organization argues. Israeli tactics are no different than those used in other Western democracies and are not in violation of international human rights standards, FLAME concludes.

The so-called "intifada," the uprising of the Arab population in the territories administered by Israel, has been going on since October 2000. In that time, over 350 Arabs, mostly young people, have been killed and many have been wounded. The U.S. State Department, in its Report on Human Rights, has been critical of some aspects of Israel's human rights posture.

A Society Based on Law

Israel is a society based on law. Every measure taken by civilian or military authorities is scrutinized by the country's legal authorities. In dealing with the "intifada," Israel is faced with a difficult problem—the uprising of a civilian population. This is a problem very similar to that faced by the British in Northern Ireland, by the Filipinos in its southern islands and the Spanish in the Basque provinces. Responsible government has the obligation to maintain order and to preserve law and to do so with as little loss of life and with as little injury to the civilian population as possible.

Israel has done just that. The loss of over 350 Arab lives is of course a tragedy—every human life is precious. But seen in context, the number of casualties is really very small and a reflection on the care and restraint of the Israeli military. Israeli soldiers are confronted daily with violent riots—massive stoning and fire bombing of persons and moving vehicles, attacks with iron bars, chains, knives, Molotov cocktails and other lethal weapons. Such violence is meant to kill. Israeli soldiers and civilians have lost their lives. Almost 1,300 Israelis have been injured, some of them critically.

The task of the IDF (Israeli Defense Forces) is made more difficult by the tactics of the Arabs in having their able-bodied adult men stay behind and having their children and their women confront the IDF. It is a no-win situation for the Israelis. They try to avoid death and injury at all cost. But death and injury are sometimes unavoidable in riot situations. Since Israel is an open society, reporters and television crews from all around the world have access to the happenings, quite a few of which are staged for their benefit. Obviously it is a public relations disaster for the Israelis to have the world see their troops confronting women and children. Those women and children, however, wish to inflict as much damage as they possibly can. They mean to kill.

Maintaining Law and Order

The IDF, one of the finest armies in the world, is trained to defend the country's borders, and not for riot control. Therefore, almost inevitably, errors were made in the initial phases of the uprising. But from the very beginning, detailed instructions were given to the troops on how to react to any given provocation. The orders under which Israeli military personnel operate are specific and well known to every soldier. Those who break the rules are subject to military trial and punishment. The principles of restraint and gradual response are applied. Tear gas is used to control riots. Live bullets are fired only in life-threatening situations. But to some, every means of control not used by the Israelis, including police batons or rubber or plastic bullets, is objectionable.

Those residents of the territories who are suspected to have committed serious security offenses are dealt with in full accordance with international law and the humanitarian provisions of the Geneva Conventions. All residents have full access to the Israeli legal system—even to the Israeli Supreme Court. Prisons are unhappy places in every society. But Israeli prisons and detention centers in which those arrested for security offenses are held, are fully comparable to and adhere to the standards of those in other advanced Western democracies. Certainly, not even the most rebellious Arab detainee in Israel would prefer to serve time in a Syrian, Jordanian, Iraqi or Saudi prison instead.

Within the context of massive human rights abuses throughout the Arab world, the focus on Israel seems to be entirely out of perspective. Other countries in the Middle East lack the most basic elements of human rights—freedom of speech, freedom of the press, free elections, equality for women, freedom of religion, freedom of association. Opponents, instead of facing television cameras, face execution. Those countries do not have to defend themselves against foes who are single-mindedly intent on their destruction. Yet, those nations do not draw the enormous degree of attention that Israel receives. Israel needs to adhere to its security requirements. It has an obligation to the international community to maintain law and order in the territories it administers.

Israel's Military Actions Against Palestinians Are Unwarranted

Edward W. Said

According to Edward W. Said, Israeli attempts to root out Palestinian terrorist networks are a thinly veiled excuse for destroying Palestinian society and taking over Palestinian land. While Said is opposed to such terror tactics as suicide bombings, he maintains that Israel's retaliatory measures have included the indiscriminate murder of hundreds of innocent Palestinian civilians. Said argues that Israeli attacks on Palestinian towns are designed to eliminate the infrastructure necessary to the existence of an independent Palestinian state. The Palestinians have been willing to accept land partition as a condition for peace, he insists, but the Israeli government has refused to cease its occupation of Palestinian territories. Said concludes that instead of focusing on Palestinian terrorism, the international community should pressure Israel to accept a sovereign Palestinian state. Said is a professor of English and comparative literature at Columbia University in New York. His books include *After the Last Sky: Palestinian Lives* and *The Politics of Dispossession: The Struggle for Palestinian Self-Determination, 1969–1994.*

Despite Israel's effort to restrict coverage of its destructive invasion of the West Bank's Palestinian towns and refugee camps, information and images have nevertheless seeped through. The Internet has provided hundreds of verbal as well as pictorial eyewitness reports, as have Arab and European TV coverage, most of it unavailable or blocked or spun out of existence from the mainstream US media. That evidence provides stunning proof of what Israel's campaign has actually—has always—been about: the irreversible conquest of Palestinian land and society. The official line (which Washington has basically supported, along with nearly every US media commentator) is that Israel has been defending itself by retaliating against the suicide bombings that have undermined its security and even threatened its

Edward W. Said, "What Israel Has Done: Seeking to Eliminate the Palestinians as a People, It Is Destroying Their Civil Life," *Nation*, vol. 274, May 6, 2002, p. 20. Copyright © 2002 by The Nation Magazine/The Nation Company, Inc. Reproduced by permission.

existence. That claim has gained the status of an absolute truth, moderated neither by what Israel has done nor by what in fact has been done to it.

Phrases such as "plucking out the terrorist network," "destroying the terrorist infrastructure" and "attacking terrorist nests" (note the total dehumanization involved) are repeated so often and so unthinkingly that they have given Israel the right to destroy Palestinian civil life, with a shocking degree of sheer wanton destruction, killing, humiliation and vandalism.

Destroying Palestinian Civil Life

There are signs, however, that Israel's amazing, not to say grotesque, claim to be fighting for its existence is slowly being eroded by the devastation wrought by the Jewish state and its homicidal prime minister, Ariel Sharon. Take this front-page *New York Times* report, "Attacks Turn Palestinian Plans Into Bent Metal and Piles of Dust," by Serge Schmemann (no Palestinian propagandist) on April 11, 2002: "There is no way to assess the full extent of the damage to the cities and towns—Ramallah, Bethlehem, Tulkarm, Qalqilya, Nablus and Jenin—while they remain under a tight siege, with patrols and snipers firing in the streets. But it is safe to say that the infrastructure of life itself and of any future Palestinian state—roads, schools, electricity pylons, water pipes, telephone lines—has been devastated."

By what inhuman calculus did Israel's army, using dozens of tanks and armored personnel carriers, along with hundreds of missile strikes from US-supplied Apache helicopter gunships, besiege Jenin's refugee camp for over a week, a one-square-kilometer patch of shacks housing 15,000 refugees and a few dozen men armed with automatic rifles and no missiles or tanks, and call it a response to terrorist violence and a threat to Israel's survival? There are reported to be hundreds buried in the rubble, which Israeli bulldozers began heaping over the camp's ruins after the fighting ended. Are Palestinian civilian men, women and children no more than rats or cockroaches that can be attacked and killed in the thousands without so much as a word of compassion or in their defense? And what about the capture of thousands of men who have been taken off by Israeli soldiers, the destitution and homelessness of so many ordinary people trying to survive in the ruins created by Israeli bulldozers all over the West Bank, the siege that has now gone on for months and months, the cutting off of electricity and water in Palestinian towns, the long days of total curfew, the shortage of food and medicine, the wounded who have bled to death, the systematic attacks on ambulances and aid workers that even the mild-mannered [UN Secretary-General] Kofi Annan has decried as outrageous? Those actions will not be pushed so easily into the memory hole. Its friends must ask Israel how its suicidal policies can possibly gain it peace, acceptance and security.

Israel's Actions Are Not Justified

The monstrous transformation of an entire people by a formidable and feared propaganda machine into little more than militants and terrorists has allowed not just Israel's military but its fleet of writers and defenders to efface a terrible history of injustice, suffering and abuse in order to destroy the civil existence of the Palestinian people with impunity. Gone from public memory are the destruction of Palestinian society in 1948 and the creation of a dispossessed people; the conquest of the West Bank and Gaza and their military occupation since 1967; the invasion of Lebanon in 1982, with its 17,500 Lebanese and Palestinian dead and the Sabra and Shatila massacres; the continuous assault on Palestinian schools, refugee camps, hospitals, civil installations of every kind. What antiterrorist purpose is served by destroying the building and then removing the records of the ministry of education; the Ramallah municipality; the Central Bureau of Statistics; various institutes specializing in civil rights, health, culture and economic development; hospitals, radio and TV stations? Isn't it clear that Sharon is bent not only on breaking the Palestinians but on trying to eliminate them as a people with national institutions?

In such a context of disparity and asymmetrical power it seems deranged to keep asking the Palestinians, who have no army, air force, tanks or functioning leadership, to renounce violence, and to require no comparable limitation on Israel's actions. It certainly obscures Israel's systematic use of lethal force against unarmed civilians, copiously documented by all the major human rights organizations. Even the matter of suicide bombers, which I have always opposed, cannot be examined from a viewpoint that permits a hidden racist standard to value Israeli lives over the many more Palestinian lives that have been lost, maimed, distorted and foreshortened by long-standing military occupation and the systematic barbarity openly used by Sharon against Palestinians since the beginning of his career.

Israel Must Accept a Palestinian State

There can be no conceivable peace that doesn't tackle the real issue, which is Israel's utter refusal to accept the sovereign existence of a Palestinian people that is entitled to rights over what Sharon and most of his supporters considered to be the land of Greater Israel, i.e., the West Bank and Gaza. A profile of Sharon in the April 5, 2002, *Financial Times* concluded with this telling extract from his autobiography, which the *FT* prefaced with, "He has written with pride of his parents' belief that Jews and Arabs could be citizens side by side." Then the relevant passage from Sharon's book: "But they believed without question that only they had rights over the land. And no one was going to force them out, regardless of terror or anything else. When the land belongs to you physically . . . that is when you have power, not just physical power but spiritual power."

In 1988 the Palestine Liberation Organization (PLO) made the concession of accepting partition of Palestine into two states. This was reaffirmed on numerous occasions, and certainly in the Oslo documents. But only the Palestinians explicitly recognized the notion of partition. Israel never has. This is why there are now more than 170 settlements on Palestinian land, why there is a 300-mile road network connecting them to each other and totally impeding Palestinian movement (according to Jeff Halper of The Israeli Committee Against House Demolitions, it costs $3 billion and has been funded by the United States), and why no Israeli prime minister has ever conceded any real sovereignty to the Palestinians, and why the settlements have grown on an annual basis. The merest glance at the map reveals what Israel has been doing throughout the peace process, and what the consequent geographical discontinuity and shrinkage in Palestinian life has been. In effect, Israel considers itself and the Jewish people to own all of Palestine. There are land ownership laws in Israel itself guaranteeing this, but in the West Bank and Gaza the settlements, roads and refusal to concede sovereign land rights to the Palestinians serve the same function.

What boggles the mind is that no official—no US, no Palestinian, no Arab, no UN, no European, or anyone else—has challenged Israel on this point, which has been threaded through all of the Oslo agreements. Which is why, after nearly ten years of peace negotiations, Israel still controls the West Bank and Gaza. They are more directly controlled by more than 1,000 Israeli tanks and thousands of soldiers today, but the underlying principle is the same. No Israeli leader (and certainly not Sharon and his Land of Israel supporters, who are the majority in his government) has either officially recognized the occupied territories as occupied or gone on to recognize that Palestinians could or might theoretically have sovereign rights—that is, without Israeli control over borders, water, air or security—to what most of the world considers Palestinian land. So to speak about the vision of a Palestinian state, as has become fashionable, is a mere vision unless the question of land ownership and sovereignty is openly and officially conceded by the Israeli government. None ever has and, if I am right, none will in the near future. It should be remembered that Israel is the only state in the world today that has never had internationally declared borders; the only state not the state of its citizens but of the whole Jewish people; the only state where more than 90 percent of the land is held in trust for the use only of the Jewish people. That Israel has systematically flouted international law . . . suggests the depth and structural knottiness of the absolute rejectionism that Palestinians have had to face.

Israel Must Make Concessions

This is why I have been skeptical about discussions and meetings about peace, which is a lovely word but in the present context usually means Palestinians are told to stop resisting Israeli control over their land. It is among the many deficiencies of Arafat's terrible leadership (to say nothing of the even more lamentable Arab leaders in general) that he neither made the decade-long Oslo negotiations ever focus on land ownership, thus never putting the onus on Israel to declare itself willing to give up title to Palestinian land, nor asked that Israel be required to deal with any of its responsibility for the sufferings of his people. Now I worry that he may simply be trying to save himself again, whereas what we really need are international monitors to protect us, as well as new elections to assure a real political future for the Palestinian people.

The profound question facing Israel and its people is this: Is it willing to assume the rights and obligations of being a country like any other, and forswear the kind of impossible colonial assertions for which Sharon and his parents and soldiers have been fighting since day one? In 1948 Palestinians lost 78 percent of Palestine. In 1967 they lost the remaining 22 percent. Now the international community must lay upon Israel the obligation to accept the principle of real, as opposed to fictional, partition, and to accept the principle of limiting Israel's extraterritorial claims, those absurd, biblically based pretensions and laws that have so far allowed it to override another people. Why is that kind of fundamentalism unquestioningly tolerated? But so far all we hear is that Palestinians must give up violence and condemn terror. Is nothing substantive ever demanded of Israel, and can it go on doing what it has without a thought for the consequences? That is the real question of its existence, whether it can exist as a state like all others, or must always be above the constraints and duties of other states. The record is not reassuring.

RELIGIOUS EXTREMISM: A PROBLEM ON BOTH SIDES

Allan C. Brownfeld

Allan C. Brownfeld is a syndicated columnist and the editor of *Issues*, the quarterly journal of the American Council for Judaism. In the following selection, Brownfeld takes issue with the belief that Islamic extremists are the only religious fundamentalists who commit acts of violence in the Middle East. He cites several examples of deadly terrorist attacks against Palestinians that were perpetrated by orthodox Jewish extremists who justified their actions as being part of a holy war for the land of Israel. These violent extremists are tolerated—or even tacitly supported—by many Israeli religious and secular leaders, Brownfeld writes. The author acknowledges that Palestinian terrorists are also motivated by the idea that they are fighting a holy war. Religious extremism on both sides of the conflict needs to be confronted, Brownfeld asserts, if a peaceful solution is ever to be found.

The Sept. 11, 2001, terrorist attacks against the U.S. have, quite properly, focused attention upon the religious extremism which motivated the suicide bombers of al-Qaeda. All too often, religious schools in Saudi Arabia, Pakistan and a number of other countries have confused religion and politics and have promoted a form of Islamic fundamentalism which sees those of other faiths—and, in particular, the West—as eternal enemies.

Yet, those who speak of a "clash of cultures" between the West and the Islamic world tend to forget that religious fundamentalism comes in many forms, and can be found in many traditions. In recent years Christian leaders, both Catholic and Protestant, have apologized for the brutality of the Crusades and of inquisitions which they committed in the name of religion. Even today, there are fundamentalist Christians who promote the most extreme policies with regard to the Middle East in anticipation of the final Battle of Armaggedon which such policies might provoke.

Within Judaism, as well, we have seen religious fundamentalism and extremism which has led, among other things, to the assassina-

Allan C. Brownfeld, "Religious Extremism and Holy War: Jews as Well as Muslims Must Put House in Order," *Washington Report on Middle East Affairs*, vol. 21, March 2002, p. 85. Copyright © 2002 by American Educational Trust. Reproduced by permission.

tion of Israeli Prime Minister Yitzhak Rabin because of his efforts to move toward peace with the Palestinians.

Rabin's assassin, Yigal Amir, brought the largely unknown and unreported world of Israel's religious extremists under public scrutiny. "These are true believers," said Ehud Sprinzik, a professor at Hebrew University in Jerusalem and a leading Israeli expert on the radical right. "They believe it was God, not so much the Israeli army, but the hand of God that gave them back these lands in 1967. It was God sending a message that he was ready to redeem them. They have built a world of Torah, with Yeshivas, schools, a religious lifestyle. Now this is committing a huge religious sin, a sin against God. . .".

Acts of violence by religious zealots in Israel have been increasing. In September 1995, Jewish settlers stormed a Palestinian girls' school in Hebron, beat its headmistress and injured at least four pupils who took part in a street protest. A municipal spokesman said, "The school is about 20 yards from a Jewish settlement. Some settlers attacked the school and tried to get rid of the Palestinian flag on it. They attacked the headmistress, and even the little girls there, with bottles and pipes."

In another incident, five armed men in Israeli army uniforms, some of them masked, terrorized Halhoul, an Arab village on the West Bank, forcing their way into private houses and interrogating the Palestinians they met. They shot one young man to death as his father watched, bound at the hands and helpless to intercede. Responsibility for the killing was claimed by Eyal, a spinoff of the late Meir Kahane's Kach movement—the same group implicated in the Rabin assassination.

Among the most traumatic acts of violence was the February 1994 massacre of 29 Palestinians at the Tomb of the Patriarchs in Hebron. Baruch Goldstein, an American-born physician and ultra-right-wing Israeli settler, gunned them down as they worshiped.

Goldstein, a militant Zionist from New York, had been a member of the Jewish Defense League (JDL), founded by the late Meir Kahane, who urged his followers to emigrate to Israel and called for the removal of all Arabs from the West Bank. After the violent mass murder at Hebron, Goldstein was viewed as a hero by many of the Israeli settlers. At his funeral, Rabbi Yaacov Perrin declared that "one million Arabs are not worth a Jewish fingernail." Samuel Hacohen, a teacher in a Jerusalem college, said: "Baruch Goldstein was the greatest Jew alive, not in one way, but in every way. . . . There are no innocent Arabs here. . . . He was no crazy. . . . Killing isn't nice, sometimes it is necessary."

In the eyes of Jewish religious fundamentalists, Yitzhak Rabin committed the ultimate act of betrayal when he signed an agreement in the peace process ceding much of the West Bank of the Jordan River— what the Bible calls the lands of Judea and Samaria—to the Palestinians, and thus also ceding any imminent prospect of creating Greater

Israel. His assassin, Yigal Amir, told authorities God had ordered him to kill Rabin.

An Increase in Israeli Extremism

The intolerance of Israel's religious fundamentalists has been growing for many years. Both the Israeli government and leaders in the American Jewish community have repeatedly downplayed the dangers of such movements. Recalling an earlier visit to Israel, *Washington Post* columnist Richard Cohen wrote: "Back in 1980, Rabbi Moshe Levinger, a major force in the Israeli settlements movement, led me through the market at Hebron, wading through Arabs with a contempt and disdain that I found both repulsive and downright scary. Levinger acted as if God has ensured his safety. I, however, had not gotten such a message. Levinger is an important figure for a number of reasons. In the first place, the settlement he and his wife, Miriam, established in Hebron was clearly illegal. The government moved to protect it anyway, and, ultimately, provided it with utilities. Second, Levinger was later convicted of killing an unarmed Arab in a burst of anger—and served no more than 10 weeks in jail. In other words, Levinger has been the personification of the Israeli government's refusal to come to grips with extremists. Some politicians admire them; others merely want their votes."

Amos Oz, Israel's most celebrated writer, refers to his country's extremists as "Hezbollah in a skullcap." He says that Rabin's death made him realize that "the real battle in the Middle East is no longer between Arabs and Jews but between fanatics of both faiths and the rest of the people in the Middle East who want to find some reasonable compromise." He states that, "Compromise is synonymous with life itself" and that "the opposite of compromise is not integrity but suicide and death."

Writing in the *Los Angeles Times* Israeli journalist Yossi Melman notes that, "Dr. Baruch Goldstein was no exception. . . . He was preceded by Elliot Goodman and Craig Latner. In April 1982, Goodman, of Tenafly, New Jersey, stormed into the El Omar mosque on Temple Mount in Jerusalem and fired into a Palestinian crowd. Miraculously, 'only' two worshippers were killed and 11 wounded. . . . Two years later, Latner and three colleagues, all from Jewish neighborhoods in New York, opened fire on a bus carrying Palestinian workers near the same city. Five were injured. . . . Successive Israeli governments . . . regarded these incidents as isolated, refusing to admit they were products of a larger psychological environment—the Jewish settlers' movement that had nourished Palestinian hatred. The Israeli government is now paying the price of this accommodating attitude toward Jewish extremism."

Rabbi Uri Regev, director of Reform Judaism's Israel Religious Action Center, warns that the terrorist attacks of Sept. 11 should make clear the need to fight against both Israeli and Palestinian "zealots."

In a talk at Anshe Chesed Fairmount Temple in Cleveland shortly after Sept. 11, Regev accused the Israeli Orthodox establishment of limiting religious freedom by fighting any attempt to grant state recognition to Reform and Conservative conversions or weddings. Individual members of the Orthodox community, he said, had vandalized Reform and Conservative religious institutions.

In his talk, which was reported in the *Cleveland Jewish News*, Regev spoke out about the dangers of Islamic terrorism. "In Israel," he added, "we have our own religious extremists who feel they have the right to rule other people's lives, spreading the venom of fundamentalism."

Regev asserted that some fervently Orthodox Jewish leaders in Israel have used hate-filled and violent language not only against non-Jews but against liberal and secular Jews and their institutions. He expressed particular concern about a Sept. 7, 2001, article in the Israeli edition of the Orthodox newspaper *Yated He'eman* which described Reform and Conservative Jews as "destroyers of religion," "criminals," and "enemies of God."

He also pointed to a 1996 sermon by one of Israel's chief rabbis, Eliyahu Bakshi-Doren, in which he defended the violence of the biblical zealot Pinchas, and suggested that bloodshed in defense of Judaism is "like a doctor who spreads blood with his scalpel, but saves the patient."

"We need to band together to fight religious zealots on both the Palestinian and Israeli sides," Regev concluded. "If we don't learn from the Sept. 11 loss of human lives, we haven't learned anything."

Reviving the Idea of a Jewish Holy War

Writing in the December 2001 issue of the Jewish journal *Sh'ma*, Reuven Firestone, professor of medieval Judaism and Islam at Hebrew Union College in Los Angeles and author of, among other works, *Children of Abraham: An Introduction to Judaism for Muslims*, declared: "Before dismissing the appalling behaviors of our Muslim cousins engaged in holy war, let us put our own house in order. Holy war has been revived among Israel the people and within Israel the state. . . . After the Mishnah [an interpretation of the Talmud], Jewish holy war ideas lay virtually dormant . . . though they were discussed briefly by certain medieval thinkers and appear in some of our apocalyptic and messianic writings. But holy war has been revived in contemporary Israel, especially among ultranationalist Orthodox settlers in Judea and Samaria (the West Bank) and their many supporters. The war—and it may now be accurately called a war between Israel and the Palestinians—is defined by many religiously observant settlers and their supporters as a divine obligation to reclaim the whole of the Land of Israel as either a prelude to or actually part of the messianic awakening."

Dr. Firestone noted that, "Many in this camp cite ad nauseum the now famous statement of Nahmanides [a medieval Jewish scholar and commentator] in his gloss on [medieval Jewish philosopher] Maimonides' Book of Commandments (positive commandment 4), who teaches that the conquest and settlement of the Land of Israel lies in the category of obligatory war (milhemet mitzvah). 'It is a positive commandment for all generations obligating every individual, even during the period of exile.' As Jewish holy war has entered religious and political discourse in relation to the Israel-Palestine conflict, so has the increase of Jewish atrocities in the name of a higher cause. It reached its peak in the mid-1980s to mid-1990s with the maiming and murdering of Muslim noncombatants by the Jewish Underground, the massacre of Muslims in prayer by Baruch Goldstein, and Yigal Amir's assassination of Prime Minister Yitzhak Rabin. Holy war ideas continue to inform the behavior of many religious settlers to this day. . . ."

While there has been much attention paid in recent days to the advocates of "holy war" within the Islamic community—as well there should be—insufficient attention has been paid to similar movements within Judaism, particularly by national Jewish organizations which traditionally have ignored the extremists within the Jewish community while doing their best to highlight the misdeeds of similar extremists in other communities.

Reuven Firestone concluded by stating that, "Holy war is a dangerous reality. We have now felt its sting. Let us, therefore, before we try vainly and patronizingly to intervene in the internal debates of another religious community, put our own house in order. We must neutralize if not eradicate the ugly and gravely dangerous revival of holy war within Judaism. The first step is to acknowledge its existence. The next is to engage in public discussion within our own community, especially among the spectrum of religious leaders, to mitigate the inherently self-destructive and ultimately immoral efforts to define our fighting with Palestinians as a holy war."

Lonely Voices

Uri Regev and Reuven Firestone are somewhat lonely voices. In the book *Murder in the Name of God: The Plot to Kill Yitzhak Rabin*, Michael Karpin, one of Israel's leading journalists, and Ina Friedman, an American-born editor, journalist and translator in Israel, point out that in the wake of the Rabin assassination, Israeli society refused to properly confront the forces which brought it about. The commission headed by Meir Shamgar to investigate Rabin's murder "held back from scrutinizing the factors responsible. . . . In effect, the report reduced the murder of a prime minister from a complex historical event to a simple lapse in security arrangements. . . . Justice Shamgar had taken a similarly restrictive approach to circumstances two years earlier when he had chaired the commission investigating Baruch Goldstein's massacre. . . . In that instance too the panel confined itself to a strict elucidation of the facts and performance of the security personnel, rather than an examination of the religious, social and political conditions that had fueled the attack."

Sadly, Israel's problems are not unique. Religious extremists have been brutally slaughtering their opponents "in the name of God" from the beginning of recorded history. It is the responsibility of men and women of goodwill of all faiths to fight the bigotry within their own religious communities. This is true for Catholics and Protestants in Northern Ireland—for Hindus and Muslims in India and Pakistan—for the different faiths in the Balkans—and for those who have used the name of God as a cause for war in the Middle East. Judaism, as we have seen, is not immune from such extremism—which, finally, must be confronted.

CHAPTER 3

LIVING WITH THE ARAB-ISRAELI CONFLICT

FIVE DAYS IN THE MIDDLE EAST

Time

On September 28, 2000, Ariel Sharon, then a member of the Israeli Parliament, made headlines by visiting the al-Aqsa Mosque (also called the Temple Mount), a site held sacred by Palestinians and Jews alike. Many commentators believe that his visit—during which he was accompanied by one thousand armed guards—and his provocative speech at the holy site constituted a deliberate attempt to stir up controversy, and his actions did incite fresh outbreaks of violent protests among enraged Palestinians. Shortly after Sharon's visit to the mosque, the staff of *Time* magazine asked eight people on various sides of the conflict to record their personal reactions to the sudden escalation of tensions in Israel. In the following selection, the eight diarists express their emotions of sorrow, resignation, and anger as violence explodes around them.

Monday

Atara Triestman, 35, is a dance therapist who lives in Jerusalem with husband Yoni, son Amior, 3, and daughter Shefa, 18 months. In some ways it seems that life continues as usual, and I'm trying to feel strength from the routine, but the truth is, life hasn't been normal at all. When the rioting started, I thought I'd better stock up on food and formula in case we need to go down to the bomb shelters. I went to buy diapers today, and they were almost completely sold out—I guess everyone thought the same thing. I bought diapers that were two sizes too big. Better to have them around, just in case.

Last night we visited friends in Elazar [a moderate settlement near Jerusalem in the West Bank]. I asked my husband to call first and make sure the roads were open and it was safe to drive there. The friend in Elazar said it was, but this morning we heard on the news that a woman driving that road got stoned and was in the hospital. It's not clear if she will live. This morning, I wanted to visit friends in [another settlement called] Efrat, but I was too scared to go. The roads aren't safe anymore. Especially the tunnel road that you take to Efrat. There are two tunnels. If the Palestinians cut you off between the tunnels, it's like a siege. There's nowhere to go. Bethlehem is right nearby, and you could get lynched.

In the evening I went to the bat mitzvah of the daughter of my childhood friend. My friend said she considered canceling the bat mitzvah because of all the rioting but decided that she would be giving them—the Arabs—a victory. I sat at a table with two friends. The first lives in Givon, past Ramot on the edge of Jerusalem, right near Ramallah. She said that after the lynching, she took her three children and moved in with her mother. She took everything that was valuable to her—photographs and jewelry—because she was afraid the house might get ransacked. It struck me that where she lives is not a stereotypical religious settlement. Givon is basically secular and affluent.

I'm not a person who panics easily. Many of the people I know are totally panicked, but I try to remain calm. Maybe it's denial.

Still, I've started to think what I would take with me if I needed to evacuate the house. My friend just called from her office in Jerusalem and can't get home to Efrat because the roads are closed. She might have to sleep over here with us. That means there was probably stoning on that road.

Danny Yatom, 55, is Prime Minister Ehud Barak's Chief of Staff. He traveled with Barak to the summit [in August 2001]. We were at the office in Jerusalem Sunday night and stayed there until 2 A.M. We had to make a lot of preparations for the summit. There were discussions led by the Prime Minister, and I had to lead discussions to prepare the discussions at the prime-ministerial level. I got home in Tel Aviv at 3 A.M., and I had to wake up at 5:15 A.M. At 6:30 we were at the airport. Even onboard the airplane the schedule of the summit was not yet fixed. I had talked all night long with the Americans from the White House and with [U.S. ambassador to Israel] Martin Indyk. We had to arrange everything on the move. After the frustrations we had in [a meeting with Arafat and Secretary of State Madeleine Albright in] Paris, there was no sense of anxiety. I felt as if we were heading toward something very, very important, but my expectations were very low.

We used the one-hour flight to Egypt to make the last preparations. We landed, and immediately we were taken to the conference center, and the Prime Minister met the President of Egypt [Hosni Mubarak]. It was very clear that Mubarak wanted very much to succeed at the summit. "We can't afford a failure," he said. "It would have a very negative effect."

The second meeting was with King Abdullah [of Jordan]. Prime Minister Barak and King Abdullah have very good chemistry. They speak one to the other in a very frank way, and they trust each other very much. You can tell it by looking at them. There was an understanding that together with Jordan, we'd get a positive result. Between the meetings, I used the opportunity to meet my good friend Omar

Suleiman, who is head of Egypt's security services, and Samih Batikhi, who heads Jordan's security services. They are very, very effective. Everybody gets acquainted to good things very quickly, so I don't think of the fact that once they were my enemies.

As we headed toward evening, after dinner, the impression that started to prevail was that it would end negatively. But I must say that I felt intuitively all the time that the summit would end positively. It became clear though that we'd not get something actually signed. We spoke at the end of Monday about a presidential statement. The Americans said it would have the same effect as a signed document, because the sides would have to fulfill their commitments.

Moria Shlomot, 31, is Director of Peace Now, the biggest Israeli peace group. She lives in Tel Aviv with her daughter Tamar, 2½, and her partner, actor Chen Alon. 6:01 A.M. I am alone in the car. I am driving. There is a masked man in front of me, and he shoots in my direction. The windshield shatters. The bullet will soon reach me. How is it that this man did not see the PEACE stickers on my car? I wake up. I am alive. I am in bed. I don't usually dream such realistic dreams.

8:01. I haven't gone out yet. I haven't tidied the house yet. I haven't chosen what to wear. It looks warm to me.

9:01. At the traffic light, I am honking at the person in front of me, who is honking at the person in front of him. A friend calls from Gaza. For a moment we are pleasant and polite. Then begins the argument. We are friends more than we are enemies. Friendship in siege.

1:01 P.M. I go out to load the truck with signs to be sent to Jerusalem. On the signs it says in Arabic and in Hebrew YES TO COEXISTENCE, NO TO VIOLENCE. Because of the hurried printing, the black bleeds onto the red. I still have to bring Tamar's chair to her class. I haven't eaten yet.

2:01. Near the airport the setting changes. Clouds. Lightning. Thunder. I am wearing a short pink tank top. The editor of the local newspaper of Kibbutz Bar Am, where I was born, calls up and asks to interview me about the situation. Oh, boy, the situation. How I like to talk about the situation. There is a terrible hailstorm, and I am screaming on the telephone. I can't hear myself. I can't see anything. About three months ago, when Barak was at Camp David, we thought we were winning. That our struggle for peace was on the verge of success. That there is a chance, a future, that all this would happen during our lifetime.

8:01. I arrived home after Tamar had already gone to bed. There is no peace, and on top of that, I am a lousy mother.

Tuesday

Sheik Jamal Tawil, 40, is the Imam of the Grand Mosque in Beituniya, a district of Ramallah in the West Bank. In the name of God the merciful, the compassionate. I woke up at dawn. I did my ablutions before the prayer. I was about to leave for the mosque to lead the prayer. My wife tried to persuade me not to go. The Moustaribine [Israeli undercover forces disguised as Arabs] had sneaked into our neighborhood. We prayed at home. I switched on the TV. There were clashes near the settlement at Tawil Mountain, called by the occupiers Psagot [a Jewish settlement]. The children woke up. I wanted to take them to school. I gave my son Abdullah his pocket money. We left. My other son came to tell me that the city of Ramallah was under closure. Teachers and most students were not able to arrive home. We went back.

At noon I prayed at the mosque. After the prayer a march started and went through the city of Ramallah and al-Bireh. The protesters condemned the Sharm el-Sheikh accord [an agreement outlined on October 17, 2000, that called for a cease-fire and monitoring of the peace process]. The protesters arrived at the confrontation line. The occupation soldiers attacked them. We heard youths asking for help. We did not hear the sounds of gunfire. The Israeli soldiers used guns with silencers. We were unable to do the late-afternoon prayer in a mosque, so we prayed in the open. We tried to avoid being shot by snipers at the City Inn Hotel and the building next to it. After sunset, quiet prevailed. We went to the mosque and performed the evening prayer. After that we went to visit the wounded.

The government hospital was crowded with people. The administration of the hospital announced the death of Ismail Shamlakh. He was from the Gaza Strip. He came with his brother to work in the West Bank a few months ago. He was unable to see his pregnant wife, whom he left in Gaza. His son will be born as an orphan. Mourners came to pay their respects to his brother. "You should come to congratulate me," he said. "My brother wanted to be a martyr."

Danny Yatom During the night I slept 15 minutes on the couch in the Prime Minister's suite. The Prime Minister went into the bedroom. I and his personal assistant, Eldad Yaniv, took a couch each. Then we were called again to meet President Clinton at 4 A.M. Tuesday. For the first time, we learned that there was going to be a deal.

We had to go back and forth from the conference center, where the meetings were held, to the hotel. Whenever we came back, always the Egyptian security people checked us in a very, very tight way. What caused me a lot of frustration was the fact that while they were checking us, I saw the Palestinians going back and forth without anyone checking them. I felt very bad about that, because I had a badge as a member of the delegation. It happened that I had to go with my briefcase, a brown leather case. I did not allow them to open it. "This is a briefcase with all the documents belonging to the Prime Minister of Israel, and I won't let you open it," I told them.

It took me some time to convince them. They had to go and find senior security officers, but finally they let me through. This was 4 A.M. I felt tired. For some hours, I felt very bad and very tired. But I overcame it. The result was that when we flew back in the afternoon, I don't remember even the takeoff. I fell asleep immediately on the plane, and they could barely wake me up when we landed at Ben Gurion [airport near Tel Aviv]. But it was only one hour.

Then we came to the Ministry of Defense at 5 P.M. The Prime Minister discussed how to implement the Sharm el-Sheikh agreement. I had to stay in the office until 11 P.M. I had to coordinate many things. We've done all this work, but it doesn't depend only on us. If the Palestinians don't implement their commitments the way we are implementing ours, then on Friday night we might find that the words were excellent but the implementation was a failure.

Colonel Noam Tibon, 38, is commander of the Israeli army's Hebron Brigade, 2,000 soldiers based in the West Bank town of Hebron. Six A.M. Morning envelops Hebron. I hear the muezzin as on every morning with his call to prayer. The latest reports from the summit testify to a night full of crises, lack of confidence, as well as uncertainty, which directly influences what is happening in this city. Hebron is the only city in Judea and Samaria where Jews and Palestinians live together, where a city of contrasts and extremes arises to another day of confrontations. After the morning reports from the summit, I was preoccupied with the question of whether the Palestinians really want peace as well as whether they were capable of exerting control over the streets. I am thinking of Abu Ramzi, the Palestinian Brigade commander here, a proud and straight man. The instructions he received put him into an impossible situation, and he was compelled to allow gunfire by Tanzim activists in the direction of the Israeli Defense Forces position and the Jewish community. During our last meeting, he could not look me in the eyes. It is so hard to build trust between enemies and so easy to break it.

The morning began like every other morning, with a review of the night's events. While we were assessing the situation, my father phoned. My 70-year-old parents, who live on a kibbutz, are very worried and anxious about the situation in Israel. They went through all the wars here, but they don't stop dreaming of peace for my children, their grandchildren.

Dealing with the disturbances requires of our soldiers great professionalism and constant weighing of personal values. On the surface it looks like the confrontation between the soldier with his weaponry and the Palestinian youth who is throwing stones is in favor of the army. The dilemma for the soldier is between the orders he received, whose main principles are restraint and humanity, and the feeling of fear as a result of the thousands of rioters who are throwing stones and Molotov cocktails at him. All the while the soldier must keep his cool and see before him his values as a human being and as a soldier. Happily, thanks to the precise preparations and instructions for restraint during the events, not one Palestinian youth who was throwing stones has been killed in the sector.

In the afternoon I convened the company commanders. They are in their mid-20s, idealistic, intelligent, firm in their beliefs and happy to have this opportunity to meet. I have no doubt morale and readiness are high. At the end of the meeting, the commanders hurry back to their sectors since, as darkness descends, the Tanzim begin shooting at cars, army positions and houses.

At 9 P.M. I travel to Kiryat Arba, the largest [Jewish] city in my sector, to speak with new immigrants from Russia. The audience is made up of people who came to our country and found themselves in a reality that is strange to them. To dispel the tension, I open with a discussion about Tolstoy's *War and Peace*, which describes the war of the Russian people against the invading Napoleon. Here in our small country we do not have the wide spaces that would allow a retreat from Moscow. The tension is broken, the audience listens to what I say, which is translated into Russian.

At midnight there is a call for all the brigade commanders in the sector. During the conversation the commander tells us details of the cease-fire agreement. In the middle of the conversation, I receive reports of gunfire toward the Jewish community in Hebron. It looks as if, for the moment, the agreement does not apply to Hebron. At 2 A.M. the gunfire ceases. It is time to give final orders and go to bed.

Wednesday

Saeb Erakat is Yasser Arafat's chief negotiator and Minister of Local Government. He lives in Jericho. This morning I was really surprised when my nine-year-old son Mohammed began a determined entry into Palestinian-Israeli politics: he asked me why the father of Mohammed al-Durra, the 12-year-old boy killed in Gaza, could not protect his son from the Israeli bullets. Why did [the Israelis] kill him? These days, everybody asks me questions. My daughter Dalal, 18, asked me about her friend Asil, from [the peace group involving Israeli and Palestinian children] Seeds of Peace, who was also killed by the Israelis. Others ask me when the Israelis will lift the closure and siege. When will the airport be opened? All these questions boil down to one, put to me in words and in body language: Is this the peace you are making for us?

I have my own questions. Why are the Israelis stationed here? Why tanks? Why can't they lift the siege and move their soldiers and tanks from the entrance of Palestinian towns, villages and refugee camps? I asked Ambassador Dennis Ross, the U.S. Middle East peace coordinator, all these questions. The more questions I ask, the more I have to answer.

The farmers of Jericho requested a meeting with me. I know the impact of the siege on these farmers: they can't market their vegetables outside Jericho. Most of their crops remained uncultivated. I met with the tourism sector of Jericho, hoteliers and restaurateurs. No one is allowed to enter or leave Jericho. All hotels, restaurants, the cable car that goes up to the Mount of Temptation and the Hisham Palace are closed. This is a total devastation to me. These people voted for me. I am their representative in the Palestinian Legislative Council.

Tension is really high. It was 4 A.M. when I arrived back home. My wife Name'ah was waiting and extremely upset at me. She was screaming at me in every direction. I did not respond. I kept looking at her eyes. She was worried and confused. Then Name'ah asked very gently if I was hungry.

We cannot defend ourselves; we don't have an army, navy or an air force. Our agreements with Israel prevent us from that. Why would they do such a thing? Is it not enough to have tanks, soldiers. We already have more than 100 dead Palestinians and about 3,000 wounded. Palestinians are very angry at this development.

I think back to last week. Then, without any prior warning, the youth of Jericho were on their way to torch the city's "Peace unto Israel" synagogue, a modern structure built above a 7th century Byzantine mosaic floor depicting Jewish symbols. The synagogue is exclusively under Palestinian control. I always use it as an example of how Palestinians and Israelis must live together. I rushed to the place. There were hundreds of people in the crowd. The Palestinian security commander of Jericho was standing in the middle with about 50 policemen, trying very hard to push the crowd back. I stood next to him, held my arms outstretched and began shouting at the crowd, "Don't do that, you can't!" They shouted back, "They are killing us! They are destroying us! They don't want peace! We want them out! Go home! They don't want peace!" I tried again. "Please stop! This is madness. Please, we can't do this!" Suddenly, they stopped and began leaving. I was really surprised. The damage to the building was moderate. The mosaic floor was unharmed. I asked to see the mayor of Jericho. "Please," I told him, "I want you to begin repairing the damage immediately. Please, Mr. Mayor, I would appreciate this very much," I said. Less than one hour later, Israeli helicopters began firing missiles into Jericho. The missiles struck a police warehouse where thousands of uniforms are stored.

The missiles' real impact was not on the warehouse. This time, my son Mohammed, terrified, trembling after the blast, asked me, "Is this the peace you're making for us?" He was weeping in my arms. His tears were much more devastating to me than the Israeli missiles. This is the main reason for the peace process, the future generations of Palestinians and Israelis. I don't want Mohammed to go through what I went through in 1967. I want him to have an alternative. My soul is searching for answers. I am so confused. I am so doubtful.

Thursday

Kiyan Khaled al-Sayfi, 16, is a Palestinian schoolgirl from Dheisheh refugee camp in Bethlehem. She studies at a school in the camp run by the U.N.

Relief and Works Agency. The sun rises to begin a new day. Its golden beams mix with the breeze, which makes the tree's branches move. The sound of wind blowing against the tree's leaves is beautiful. I have a feeling of serenity. I woke up at 6 A.M. to welcome a new day, a quiet day, a happy day, unlike the other days. But, in my opinion, it will not be a happy day. We will get the same sad news. I picked up my bag and went to school. I don't have a strong desire to study. I expect to die at any moment by a stray bullet from an Israeli soldier. I looked at my house. I gazed at all the spots I used to sit on or play, as it is my last time to see them. It is a terrible feeling.

A schoolmate called me. We discussed our cause on our way to school. Everything was the same at the school: the same teachers, the same students, the textbooks, the chalkboards. We started our day by reciting poems for Palestine. The bell rang for the first class, a science lesson. The teacher entered. She began talking. I was not listening. I thought about our martyrs and wounded. I thought of the 13-year-old child who fell a martyr. How sad is his mother? I am proud of him. He was from my region. He was killed on his way back home. What is the use of what he had learned? He was killed. Did he know that he should not prepare his homework because a bullet would kill him? It is an evil bullet fired by a wicked soldier. I gazed at our teacher. I am one of her best students. But now I do not care about the lesson. Study is no longer important in our life.

After we finished our study, we went to visit the family of a martyr, to provide support. As we marched we chanted, "Rest, martyr, in your grave; we will continue the struggle. We sacrifice our soul and blood for the martyr and for Palestine." That martyr was shot by a high-velocity bullet. It penetrated his chest. Another bullet penetrated his arm. He was 18. His mother was sitting on the ground. She was crying. Her wrinkled face was furious. I kissed her face and hands.

Atara Triestman I try not to imagine the worst, although sometimes it seems I am surrounded by people who can't help being afraid. My husband Yoni is afraid. He sees Arab politicians and Muslim clergy inciting Muslims everywhere against Jews, saying that Jews deserve violence and accepting that killing Jews is a heroic mission. Today he says he sees the jihad spreading and that he cannot look into the eyes of an Arab without wondering if he could act like the mob in Ramallah that lynched the soldiers.

Friday

Qais Adwan is the chairman of the student union at An-Najah University in Nablus. He is a member of Hamas, a militant Islamic Palestinian organization. Before sunrise, the youths in the dormitory have readied themselves for the dawn prayer. Some go back to bed, others begin to study until 7 A.M. I went to the campus to do the usual things that I do every day. I am mandated by God to help the students. But on this typical day, I am thinking of a day two weeks ago, still. It was a special day in my life, a unique one. I was under a special premonition of fear and portent. We had decided to organize a march to protest the entrance of the criminal [Ariel] Sharon to al-Aqsa Mosque. After dawn, I started reading the Koran. The sun's rays were weaving a special dress of martyrdom. The sun told us, "You have a date with martyrdom." The Muslim believes in fate. God decides death and life. I read the verses that deal with martyrdom. My heart was brimful with a special feeling. It is very great to fall a martyr. The martyr has a high ranking in heaven.

There was a situation of tension at the campus. The student council declared a day of mourning. Representatives of all student blocs were called for a meeting to discuss the events and decide what to do. We decided to perform the martyrs' prayers. We contacted Sheik Bitawi [a Hamas leader in Nablus] and asked him to lead the prayer. Large numbers of students gathered in the courtyard. We started shouting, "God is most great!" I asked the students to wash their faces and hands before prayers. After the prayer, the students shouted again, "God is most great!" I looked at the faces of the youths, thinking that a serious incident would occur. It would be a different kind of march. After I finished my speech, thousands of students left the campus. It was the biggest march I have ever seen at An-Najah University. We walked for five or six kilometers, with strong determination. We swore to sacrifice our life and blood for al-Aqsa. Hundreds of the marchers rushed to the front line to clash with the soldiers. I could not forget these moments. The shooting from the Israeli soldiers was intense. It was like a battlefield. Our faith is our weapon against the soldiers, the occupiers. Two youths standing next to me were wounded. The number of casualties was large beyond expectation.

I received a call from Rafidiyah Hospital, and I was told that my roommate, Zakariya Kilani, 21, was among the martyrs. He was with me for two years. He was my brother and my friend. He was my body. I could not believe that Zakariya died. I lost my dearest friend. This is the decree of God. He told me at the mosque that he wanted to die as a martyr. I was unable to attend his funeral in Siris because of the military roadblocks. Many casualties arrived at the hospital. Five were martyrs. Youths shouted, "God is most great!" anytime they saw a martyr. The youths have become more determined to fight for al-Aqsa and Jerusalem. Heaven has opened its gates for martyrs. Honestly, though, I was shocked when Zakariya fell a martyr.

FAMILIES ON BOTH SIDES STRUGGLE WITH LOSS

Thomas Fields-Meyer

In the following selection, Thomas Fields-Meyer reports on two families—one Israeli, one Palestinian—who have both suffered the death of a child in the conflict. The Abu Eid family, who are Palestinian Christians, lost their oldest son to a sniper's bullet, Fields-Meyer explains, while the youngest daughter of the Jewish Ben Shoham family was killed in a suicide bombing. According to Fields-Meyer, both families were politically moderate until tragedy entered their lives. Since their daughter's death, the author writes, the Ben Shohams have begun to support military action against Palestinians. Likewise, the Abu Eids' anger about the Israeli occupation of their territory has only increased since the death of their son. Nevertheless, he notes, both families continue to hope that peace may someday prevail. Fields-Meyer is an associate editor for *People* magazine.

The nights are the most difficult hours for Fauz Abu Eid. The darkness brings fear and dread—and haunting memories. Night was when a sniper's bullet pierced an upstairs window in her family's pale, stone home in the West Bank village of Beit Jala in October 2001, killing her son Mousa, 19. Now Fauz, 47, spends the hours of darkness on the sofa, where her sleep is fitful at best. "I'm afraid," she says, "of soldiers breaking into the house."

Just a mile—and a world—away, in a hillside house in the Jerusalem neighborhood of Gilo, another sleepless mother battles her own thoughts. The lonely hours after dark are when Sipora Ben Shoham, 65, is flooded with recollections of her youngest daughter. Limor, 27, was sitting at the bar of Jerusalem's Moment cafe on the night of March 9, 2002, when a Palestinian carrying a hidden cache of explosives and nails blew himself up, killing Limor and 10 others. The death is so recent it still seems surreal to her mother. "I haven't really absorbed it," admits Sipora. "Maybe it didn't happen."

Yet the killing continues, and Beit Jala and Gilo—separated by a small valley and a 7-ft.-high concrete wall on Jerusalem's border—

Thomas Fields-Meyer, "Worlds Apart: Separated by Just a Mile, Two Families—One Palestinian, One Israeli—Struggle with Loss and Search for Hope," *People Weekly*, vol. 57, April 29, 2002, p. 52. Copyright © 2002 by Time, Inc. Reproduced by permission.

have become a microcosm of the conflict raging between Palestinians and Israelis. Families like the Abu Eids view the Israelis in Gilo as occupiers of land that was once in Palestinian hands. But Gilo's residents consider the land vital to the security of Israel, which captured it only after neighboring Arab nations invaded in 1967's Six-Day War.

Since then, the rift has only grown deeper and bloodier. . . . On March 29, 2002, Israeli forces, responding to months of terror attacks within Israel, began rolling into West Bank towns and cities, determined to smash the Palestinians' ability to wreak terror on Israel's civilians. Even as Secretary of State Colin Powell shuttled through the region in a desperate bid to restore calm, the carnage continued unabated. "Each death drives these communities further outside the circle of peace," says Yitzhak Frankenthal, an Israeli who runs a group for families of victims on both sides of the dispute. "Every time someone dies, it makes more hatred, bloodshed and revenge."

Losing a Son

The rage is palpable on the streets of Beit Jala, a hilly town of 13,500 where Fauz and George Abu Eid, Palestinian Christians, live in a solid two-story home built more than half a century ago by George's late father, a schoolteacher. George, 56, a housepainter who worked in Israel until the borders were sealed in October 2000, once considered himself a political moderate, and as Christians—like most of Beit Jala's residents—the Abu Eids have never been strongly aligned with the Muslim fundamentalists behind the wave of terror attacks on Israel. Still, the loss of a child—and months of violence that has claimed the lives of more than 1,400 fellow Palestinians—have taken their toll. "Israelis killed my son," says Fauz, a cook at a Greek Orthodox seminary, who has two daughters, Maysa, 18, and Mahira, 14, and a son, Issa, 6. "My children will never forget."

Mousa, recalls his mother, was "a good boy," who was studying to become an electrician and had started working part-time at construction sites three months earlier. "He was so happy to be bringing money into the house," Fauz says of her son, who instructed his mother to save the money to buy a computer for Maysa's studies. "He just wasn't political at all."

On the last afternoon of his life Mousa returned home from a shopping trip with treats for the whole family. "He said, 'I brought you the best cookies in the shop,'" recalls George. Mousa urged his family to come downstairs, where he felt they would be safer. After months of fending off fire from Palestinian gunmen—mostly Islamic militants from outside Beit Jala who have injured some 400 Gilo residents since September 2000—Israeli troops had moved snipers onto Beit Jala rooftops.

Fauz, son Issa and Mahira were downstairs playing cards around 6 P.M. when Mousa went up to get a blanket for his brother. Suddenly

Fauz heard a thump from the floor above. Moments later George discovered Mousa collapsed on the floor, blood gushing from where a bullet had pierced his neck and come out the middle of his back. Israeli military officials would say later that their sniper had fired at a gunman, but George says his son did nothing more than glance through the window of his own home. "He didn't throw stones—he wasn't out shooting," says George. "That wasn't Mousa." Little Issa rushed upstairs and "for three minutes, he watched his brother dying in a pool of blood," says George, who did his best to resuscitate his son—to no avail.

The family plunged into mourning. They placed Mousa's body in the family's black, marble-faced tomb in a cemetery at the center of Beit Jala, but with firefights on the streets outside, the Abu Eids spent most of the traditional three-day mourning period trapped in the house. Younger brother Issa was bewildered. "He didn't understand that Mousa would never come back," says sister Maysa, a student of business administration at a Bethlehem university, who has dealt with her own grief by focusing on her studies.

Under Israeli Control

For Mousa's parents, the death proved devastating. "It not only killed him—it killed me, my wife, my whole family," says George, whose home is now adorned with poster after poster bearing large photographs of Mousa and declaring him a martyr for the Palestinian cause. In a second-floor window, a small pane of glass still bears a single bullet hole. "I won't change the glass in 10 years," says George. "It is Mousa's memorial."

It also serves as a symbol of George's increasing indignation at the Israelis, who, he says, are occupying land that rightly belongs to Palestinians. George estimates that the Abu Eid family has lived in Beit Jala for some four centuries, and he resents Israeli settlers who have come from other countries, such as the former Soviet republics, to settle in Gilo. "Overnight they take it and call it theirs," he says. "Is that justice?" Though the couple say their Christian religion does not condone suicide bombing, they do not blame the bombers and gunmen who have killed 420 Israelis since the intifada began. "I see them as martyrs," says Fauz.

That sort of passionate hatred only deepened when the Israelis—pushed over the edge by the March 27, 2002, massacre of 28 people at a Passover seder in coastal Netanya—swept into the West Bank, imposing 24-hour curfews in places like Beit Jala. For days on end, the Abu Eids have been stuck close to home, keeping busy with card games, gardening, TV news and—in Fauz's case—embroidery, while the sound of gunfire and the roar of Israeli aircraft rumble almost constantly outside. "It feels like we are wasting our lives," says George. "We are prisoners in our own home."

When a friend calls on the afternoon of April 13, 2002, to share the news that the curfew has been lifted, Fauz leaps into a battered sedan driven to the market by George's brother Suhail. On the way he stops the car so Fauz can visit the local cemetery, where she makes her way to the stone bearing Mousa's name and portrait. She straightens a wooden cross, then touches Mousa's etched smile, wipes a tear from her face and walks away in silence toward the market to shop.

Minutes later Fauz is carrying a bag of five chickens from the market when explosions rock the area. Israeli troops have fired two tear-gas canisters to disperse the crowd. Quickly she jumps back in the car to head home. Asked whose side God is on in this bloody conflict, she says, "God has nothing to do with this. It comes from the brains of humans."

Losing a Daughter

On the other side of the concrete wall, another family grieves and rages, in striking symmetry with the Abu Eids. Early each morning, when taxi driver Shlomo Ben Shoham drives from Gilo to begin his shift, his first stop is at a narrow Jerusalem intersection down the block from Prime Minister Ariel Sharon's residence. At what was once the Moment cafe, Shlomo, 66, weeps as he places his daily memorial candle in memory of his daughter. "I loved her so much," he says. "My soul has been taken."

Shlomo last saw his daughter the evening of March 9, 2002, when she left the home she still shared with her parents—secular Sephardic Jews—for a night out with friends. When Shlomo saw on TV that a terrorist had just struck in Netanya, he called Limor, a copy-company accounts supervisor, on her cell phone to caution her to be careful. "She said she was okay," recalls Sipora. "She was near the prime minister's residence." For young Israelis frightened away from the cafes and bars of central West Jerusalem after a series of terror attacks, Moment—in staid, upscale Rehavia, just 100 yards from Sharon's heavily guarded official compound—had become an oasis. Just two weeks earlier Limor, single, apolitical, the center of a large group of friends, had celebrated her 27th birthday there.

That night she was waiting at the bar near the entrance for some friends to arrive when the 20-year-old bomber made his way to the packed cafe's entrance. When Shlomo, home in Gilo, heard the cafe's name on the TV, he immediately guessed the worst. "I knew she was dead," says Shlomo. In minutes a call came from one of the friends who was to meet Limor, asking where she was—and taking Sipora's last hope. "It meant she was gone," says Sipora. "I started to go crazy."

During shivah, the traditional Jewish week of mourning, friends streamed into the Ben Shohams' terraced home, and all spoke lovingly about the vivacious woman who had been lost, who loved partying and enjoyed giving friends makeovers. "She had a heart big enough to include everyone," says her brother Yaron, 36, a hospital driver. Says Sipora: "The house is so sad now."

Living with Terror

It was hardly the fate the couple had envisioned when they moved to Gilo 25 years ago. Sipora, the Jerusalem-born daughter of Syrian immigrants, and Shlomo, who immigrated with his family from Turkey at age 13, married in 1963. A construction worker, he also fought in three of Israel's wars—including the 1967 war, when Israel occupied areas that included the West Bank and Gaza. They settled near Tel Aviv but moved to Gilo in 1977. "I was born in Jerusalem and wanted to come back," says Sipora, who spent 25 years as an office worker at the nation's labor ministry.

Living close to the West Bank, the family regularly visited nearby Bethlehem to shop for furniture and hired Palestinians to tend their lush garden and to do odd jobs. "They would come by and eat and drink," says Sipora. "They were like friends."

Now, all interaction has stopped. "They send 17-year-olds to kill themselves and others," says son Benzi, 34, an army master sergeant who lives across the street from his parents. "They don't value life." The Ben Shohams have dug in their heels politically. Shlomo once supported foreign minister Shimon Peres, longtime backer of the peace process with the Palestinians. Now he backs Sharon's military actions.

Like the Abu Eids, the Ben Shohams now live in fear. Every trip to the grocery store, each visit to the bank, carries a risk of tragic consequences. "We are afraid to go out on our own streets," says Sipora. Now her grandchildren, 7 and 4 years old, play make-believe games, pretending to be ambulance dispatchers sending vehicles to suicide bombings. "It's impossible to live this way, with explosions all the time," says Benzi's 7-year-old son Roy.

Still, they do not talk about leaving Gilo or Jerusalem. "I love the country," Sipora says. "I will not leave because of terror." But after the death of Limor, peace with the Palestinians seems farther away than ever. "I am much hardened since then," says Benzi. "It is impossible to forgive them." And with each new report of terror, the wound opens anew. "I sympathize with every mother," says Sipora. "Who knows how many lives have been ruined?"

That maternal sympathy may, in the end, be the region's only hope for salvation. This, says Middle East scholar Philippa Strum, is what happened during the last intifada. "It was mothers concerned about their children who continued to talk about peace. I expect that someday they will again say, 'Enough. Let's resolve this without the bloodshed.'"

For now, though, a mile away, Fauz Abu Eid spends her afternoon reading from the Bible while the war rages outside. "It's not impossible for the three religions to live together on this land," she says. "I don't know what will happen, but I hope we will live in peace."

WHEN THE WAR HITS HOME: MOTHERS' STORIES

Matt Rees

Families on both sides of the Arab-Israeli conflict must struggle to survive amidst terror and grief, writes Matt Rees in the following selection. Mothers especially are affected, he explains, as they try to fulfill their roles as family nurturers during a time of instability and uncertainty. Rees tells the stories of six Israeli and Palestinian mothers who battle daily to overcome the often devastating fear associated with the continual violence. Some of these mothers have lost children, the author reports, while others fight to protect their children from attacks. They also struggle with feelings of hatred toward the other side, Rees notes, even as they continue to hope for a peaceful resolution to the conflict. Rees is the Jerusalem bureau chief for *Time*.

Rachel Dagan had been up all night when she entered the flower shop and asked for a bridal bouquet. The florist smiled and said, "Happy news! Mazel tov to the bride and groom." Dagan hesitated. She didn't want to speak. She didn't want to force her misery on others. But she couldn't hold back. "I'm going to put it on my daughter's grave," she said. The florist burst into tears. Dagan's daughter Danit was only 12 hours dead, killed by a suicide bomber who blew himself up beside the young woman and her fiance in a crowded Jerusalem cafe.

Dagan laid the garland on the shoveled earth that day, but a month later she still can't believe her beautiful daughter, 24, who had studied sociology and wanted to become a travel agent and who had kept a worn Alf doll on her bed, won't be celebrating her wedding next month as planned. Dagan leafs through Danit's datebook, recovered from the wreckage in Cafe Moment; she rereads text messages from Uri, Danit's fiance, on her daughter's red Nokia cell phone. "Uri loves Danit," says one. Then the last message: "Tonight at Moment. Uri."

It is a time for mothers to suffer, helplessly, desperately. When Palestinian and Israeli societies are being ripped apart by the testosterone and machismo of wartime, mothers are struggling to keep alive their nurturing role amid the loss, grief and fear. "In the stricken faces

Matt Rees, "When the War Hits Home," *Time*, vol. 159, April 29, 2002, p. 34. Copyright © 2002 by Time, Inc. Reproduced by permission.

of mothers—Palestinian mothers and Israeli mothers—the entire world is witnessing the agonizing cost of this conflict," President [George W.] Bush said [in April 2002]. It is a time when children can't be sent to school without the worry that some bomber or soldier will take their lives. It is a time for a woman to relax only when all her family is inside the home in front of her eyes. It is a time of struggle not to succumb to the hatred all around. As the menfolk kill and talk of necessary sacrifice, these women must fight battles of their own.

Rachel Dagan feels she has lost the struggle to keep her hopes alive. In her daughter's death, she blames everyone and everything: Palestinian leader Yasser Arafat for supporting terrorists; Israeli Prime Minister Ariel Sharon for failing to bring the peace he promised in his election campaign; the U.S. for urging restraint upon Israel for months and now for wanting Israel to cease its efforts to hunt down bomber cells in Palestinian towns. A few weeks after the bombing, Dagan went to see the dress her daughter had picked out at a shop on a Jerusalem street that has repeatedly been targeted by suicide bombers. Danit had told her it was going to be like Princess Diana's wedding dress. As Dagan scurried along the sidewalk, her pulse raced; she thought of dying in a bombing right there. "I don't care if I live or die," she remembers thinking. "I want to see her dress." That was one battle she won.

The Islamic Principal

Every day Fathiyeh Qawasmeh, principal of the all-girl Islamic Charitable School, allows her students to choose a subject for a lecture at the 9:30 A.M. assembly. Yesterday's address was about the importance of statistics in science, and the day before was a lesson from the Koran. Today three girls talked to their classmates about a woman in Gaza and her four children, all of whom had been killed when their donkey cart rolled over an Israeli mine near an Israeli settlement in the dunes south of Gaza City. Qawasmeh knew she had to help her 735 elementary and high school students understand. "Nobody is excluded, even a mother and her children," Qawasmeh told the assembly through the polyester veil that covers her nose and mouth. "We have to bear the situation, because God will reward our patience."

The school is funded by a charity that is linked to the Islamic Resistance Movement, Hamas, a group responsible for innumerable attacks on Israeli soldiers and civilians. In the lobby, the custodian keeps a Karl Gustav machine gun in his desk drawer. Two of the girls in Qawasmeh's school have been injured in the fighting that broke out [in 2000]. Shireen Rajabi, 8, has a scar above her right eyebrow; she says a soldier hit her with his rifle butt at a checkpoint.

When Qawasmeh isn't taking care of the girls at school, she is ministering to her own six children at home. At night they wake her with their nightmares. Last month she calmed her 11-year-old, Doa, the most fearful of her brood, when the girl awoke crying. "What's the worst thing that could happen to you?" Qawasmeh asked. "To be martyred," Doa sniffled. "What happens to martyrs?" her mother asked. Wiping her eyes, Doa thought a moment. "They go to heaven," she said, and then she smiled.

The Unsilenced Woman

The sheet music for a Brahms intermezzo is open on the Russian-made Rathke grand piano that rests in the salon. Wearing a gray sweat suit and teddy-bear slippers, Maha Shamas is fretting about how people view Palestinian women. First, it is the way foreigners interpret the ululating jubilation of Palestinian mothers whose children have died as "martyrs." To a Westerner, it looks like an unconscionable celebration of the death of a child. "Palestinian women have been dehumanized so much that people are willing to believe this," she says. "It's the ultimate racism. It assumes that Palestinian mothers don't love their children." This apparent elation at the sacrifice of a child, she says, is a ceremony forced on mothers by a society in which men decide for their women. "It's the result of so much pressure within society for a mother to fall into this ritual even if she has to eat up the grief she feels for her son."

For 10 years, Shamas has headed the Women's Center for Legal Aid and Counseling. [In 2000], the powerful sheik of Jerusalem's al-Aqsa Mosque condemned her in his Friday sermon for demanding that Palestinian courts stand up against tribal traditions that favor husbands and trample women's rights. Since the latest conflict with Israel began in the fall of 2000, the Women's Center has registered an increase in reports of family violence. With Palestinian men facing new financial pressures from the loss of jobs in Israel and suffering constant humiliation at the hands of Israeli soldiers, Shamas explains, "they take it out on the people closest to them."

Shamas fights the impulse to hate Israelis, but she has cut back on her contacts with Israeli human-rights activists, because, she says, they won't recognize the decades of Palestinian suffering. "They want to keep their national legends, but they want us to give ours up," she says. Her fear is that her children's generation will harbor an unrestrainable hatred for Israelis. "There's more anger in them," she says.

The daily degradation that feeds that anger can be witnessed right outside Shamas' window. Across a patch of dirt stands the A-Ram checkpoint, a set of concrete roadblocks and a guardhouse manned by twitchy Israeli soldiers. It's a place of humiliation and occasional brutality as Palestinians line up their cars to enter East Jerusalem.

[In March 2000,] Shamas' husband, a Brooklyn native of Lebanese descent, failed to pick up on a soldier's signals as he crossed the checkpoint and suddenly found the red laser dot of the Israeli's rifle sight dancing on his face. He was saved by his American-accented English and the U.S. passport he slowly pulled out of his pocket. "My

God, it hit me," Shamas says. "Nobody is safe. Think of the ease with which that soldier could have decided to kill." Every day her daughter Diala, 17, crosses the checkpoint to go to school. "Not every day do I have the inner strength," says Shamas, "to think about that."

The Disappointed Peacenik

Dorit Seideman's daughter Yael, 7, had been learning about the biblical Pharaoh before the Passover holiday earlier this month. Yael's school-teacher assigned her to write a letter to Pharaoh. "Dear Pharaoh, please come over for coffee," she wrote. "I'd like to ask you to bomb the Palestinians." Seideman was appalled. "Do you really want to kill them all?" she asked. "No," said Yael, "only the bad ones." Right now Israel's official policy is in line with Yael's letter, and that's disturbing to Seideman, who campaigned for the Peace Now movement until the birth of her three daughters left her with no time for activism.

These days Seideman's concerns are focused on her own family. Her daughters go to more slumber parties, since the fear of suicide bombers discourages their band from loitering as they once did in crowded malls. After a bombing, Seideman knows she has less than 10 minutes to make sure all her loved ones are safe, before the cell-phone network crashes under the weight of panicked calls. She is worried that her daughters will leave Israel when they're old enough, fleeing the violence. A suicide bomb exploded outside her daughters' youth club [in March 2002].

Most Israelis have shifted their political views rightward during the recent violence, and many have concluded that the Palestinians will never make peace with Israel. Seideman still maintains her conviction that a negotiated settlement is the only way to ensure the safety of her children. "We all know the solution is political, not military," she says. But for now it seems to Seideman that the Palestinians—even the liberal ones who built ties with Israelis—keep insisting on conces-sions without being prepared to compromise themselves. "I'm trying not to feel hatred, and I see that they are so desperate," she says. "But I don't feel any reciprocity."

The Unsettled Settler

The funeral cortege drove north toward the Israeli settlement of Ita-mar to bury a resident killed by Palestinian gunmen in an ambush. Nitza Tzameret was in the third car in the procession, behind an army-jeep escort. When the vehicles approached the Palestinian vil-lage of Kafr Khalil, shots rang out. The cars halted, and the terrified mourners poured out. Tzameret and her husband lay in a ditch at the roadside as Israeli soldiers returned fire up into the olive groves. The gun battle lasted 30 minutes.

Since then Tzameret has slept no more than two hours a night, fear-ing intruders in the settlement where she lives, which has no perimeter fence. Each time she leaves the house she fears that she too might be ambushed on the winding desert road from her home in the Jordan Valley up to Jerusalem. She puts on clean underwear in case she's injured and hospitalized; she fills the refrigerator so that there will be enough food for her family during the week they might spend mourning her. "Every day I bury myself," she says.

Tzameret's son Idan, 23, is a lieutenant in an army platoon involved in the current incursions in the West Bank. Before he goes on a mission, he calls her cell phone. "I love you very much, Mom," he says, then hangs up. Tzameret, a trained masseuse who practices the Japanese natural healing art of reiki, lights a candle next to Idan's photo and sends out energy to protect him. She draws Sanskrit symbols in the air and puts out telepathic lines to her son. Then she knows he's all right. But the reiki alone doesn't work for her. On her hip, she carries a small .22-cal. Beretta pistol in a black holster. There's a spare clip of tiny bronze bullets with copper tips in her handbag.

The day he died, Abdullah Franji, 14, was fasting in accordance with the rule followed by religious Muslims to forswear food on a Thursday. Before dawn that day last November, he sat before his mother to recite the chapter of the Koran his teacher had assigned him to memorize. "If two parties of the believers contend with one another, do ye endeavor to compose the matter between them," he recited, rocking back and forth as an aid to memory. Abdullah stumbled, and Wafa Franji, a teacher of the Koran herself, told him, "It's a little weak, Abdullah." The boy kissed her on the cheek. "This afternoon I'll recite it for you perfectly," he said, and he went off to school.

His friends went to Franji in the early afternoon. One of them pushed Abdullah's bicycle up the sandy alley to her front door in Gaza's poor Sabra neighborhood. They had heard that Abdullah was dead, shot by masked policemen from Yasser Arafat's Palestinian Authority after he joined a rally by Hamas students that had passed by his school. The policemen fired into the crowd, and Abdullah took a round in the head. But none of Abdullah's friends wanted to be the one to tell Franji that the long battle for power between Arafat and the Islamists had taken the life of her son. They told her only that he was at Shifa Hospital.

Franji found Abdullah laid out in the emergency room. She counted three stitches where doctors had sewn up the hole where the bullet had entered. There was blood all over. Someone had perfumed the boy's body, but she believed his sweet smell was, she later said, "a sign of Abdullah's acceptance by Prophet Muhammad, peace be upon him, who applies the scent of paradise." Recalling that Abdullah had still been fasting when he died, she says, "He broke his fast with Allah." The boy's family filed a suit against the Palestinian police, but Franji has no hope of justice in Arafat's corrupt legal system. Her comfort is the scent of paradise.

A Day in the Life of an Israeli Woman

Deborah French Greniman

Deborah French Greniman is the managing editor of *Nashim: A Journal of Jewish Women's Studies and Gender Issues.* In the following selection, Greniman describes a typical day of her life in Jerusalem during October 2000—one that ranges from mundane chores, like chauffeuring her son to school, to more harrowing events, such as attending the funeral of a coworker's brother killed that very morning in an incident related to the Arab-Israeli conflict. Although she strives to continue with her normal daily routine, Greniman explains that she has had to adapt to the realities of what she calls "the situation" in Israel, which makes life more difficult and dangerous for Israelis and Palestinians alike. Greniman also reports on the political differences that exist between Israelis; while she is sympathetic to the plight of the Arabs, the author finds that her friends and colleagues do not always share her views.

Two days after Yom Kippur, the day before the infamous lynching of two Israeli soldiers in Ramallah, I rise early to drive my spouse, who chairs Rabbis for Human Rights, to the meeting place from which he is to depart for a day-long trip to the North with other activists. He will visit in Haifa's Rambam (Maimonides) Hospital with Arabs injured in the riots and will pay a condolence call on a family that lost a member to the shots fired by Israeli police into the crowds. A little later, I drive one of my kids to junior high school; although he can take a bus that passes just two blocks from our house, he is nervous about waiting at the stop on Hebron Road, the main artery leading south out of Jerusalem toward Bethlehem, Gush Etzion, and Hebron. I come home, tidy up the kitchen, and listen to the news, which includes a small item about a pedestrian who was run down and killed an hour or two ago by an Arab driver near the entrance to one of the settlements; speculators say this may have been a terror attack. Then I ride my bicycle to the Israel Academy, where I work as an editor. It's a routine morning in the new reality of "the situation."

A Colleague's Loss

At around 9:30, I'm having a conversation in the hall with a colleague when another staff member interrupts us to whisper something about Kokhi, who works the telephone switchboard: something terrible has happened to her brother. A moment later Kokhi emerges, in the embrace of her closest friends at work, to wait in the corridor. An attractive young woman with jet-black hair, prominent features, and a bad smoking habit which she usually indulges in this same hallway, she is pregnant with her third child. Her family is sending someone over to break the news: her brother Alon was the man who was run over near the entrance to the settlement of Eli, where he lived, near Jerusalem's northern suburbs—the incident reported on the morning news.

After Kokhi has been led out, weeping, by another brother, we turn to the internet to try to find out more about what happened. According to an item posted by the daily paper *Yediot Aharonot*, the initial impression of the police is that the man was hit by accident. The spot where he had been standing by the roadside was known to be dangerous; visibility was poor at that hour of the morning; and the Arab driver himself, whose car overturned, was badly injured. But residents of Eli take a different view: they are certain that the driver is a terrorist who set out intentionally to kill a Jew with his car.

Different Politics

It's a Jerusalem custom to bury the dead as quickly as possible. The next few hours pass in lowered glances and somber conversations, and then all the staffers who can make it set out for the funeral. I go with my closest colleague, Zofia, in her car, and we end up taking Esther, Rachel, and Gila from the kitchen staff as well. Age, background, and education separate them from Zofia and me, but we've worked together in a small place for over fifteen years and are pretty friendly with each other. Gila, a nuggety woman in her early sixties, has often regaled me with stories of her childhood in Kurdistan and, later, her struggles to educate herself out of illiteracy while pushing her five children through school. Today, however, it's uncomfortable to listen to her. "Look how they keep on killing us, those Arabs, may their names be blotted out. We should shoot them down, push them out; they have no right to be here. It's our country, not theirs. God gave it to us." Zofia and I exchange glances in the front seats, but neither of us relishes the idea of getting into an unwinnable political argument on the way to a funeral. Esther and Rachel, however, demur: "Gila, you're overdoing it; they're not all like that."

Nosing through heavy traffic, we finally arrive at the funeral home, a large, bare structure of beige Jerusalem stone and cement. The parking lot outside is packed with cars and buses, but everyone manages to fit inside, mostly standing, a few sitting on benches around the sides. It's a mixed Jerusalem crowd, and, though Kokhi is neither religious nor Ashkenazi, I notice many national-religious looking types (distinguishable by the long skirts and hats worn by the women and the crocheted kippot worn by the men), evidently residents of the settlement where her brother lived. Zofia is looking glum as well as sorrowful. A wailing grandmother is led in, supported by a couple of younger women. Alon's young wife is there; the two small children are not.

Making a Martyr

The eulogies begin. The first one, given by the rabbi of the settlement, is what one might expect at the funeral of a young man: expressions of sorrow and loss, praise for the dead man's character, some name midrashim [scriptural interpretation]—"Alon" means oak tree, thus lending itself to images of a man rooted in his community and branching out into a new, young family. The second eulogy is given by Alon's father-in-law. "They tell us it was an accident," he begins, "but we know better. This was no accident." The eulogy continues with flowery biblical images of Jewish sacrifice and apocalypse. I sense a process taking place; this family and this settlement now have a martyr.

The eulogies finish, and the young man's body, wrapped, following Jerusalem custom, only in a tallit, is borne to the waiting hearse. We all hug Kokhi on our way out. Zofia and I consider accompanying the procession to the burial site, but our kitchen staff riders are adamant: they must get to work cleaning the Academy, and in any case it's not the custom in their communities for women to attend a burial. We pile back into the car. Waiting at a traffic light to cross Gaza Road in Rehavia, we watch a young man sweeping the entrance to a flower shop. Gila, sniffing that he's an Arab, starts muttering again: "You see? In the morning they shoot people, and in the afternoon they come to work." Esther and Rachel once more express good-natured objections: "Gila, it's not the same people. The ones who work aren't the ones who join the riots." No one wants to make an issue out of it. We arrive at the Academy, the women get to work, Zofia and I embrace, and I ride my bike home in the gathering dusk.

Violence Against Arabs

But the day's not over yet. At home I meet my spouse, Yehiel, back from the North. He tells me about his day. In Rambam Hospital, he talked to Ibrahim, a man from Nazareth with a big bullet wound in his chest. No one from the Jewish side had visited him yet, and though talking was difficult, he was glad of the opportunity to tell his story. He'd been in the tent set up in Nazareth at the contested lot near the Church of the Nativity, where the Moslems insist on their right to build a mosque. Not long ago, it was the site of violent Christian-Moslem clashes. Now, some kids had run into the tent seeking refuge from the police. Ibraham came out to see what was happening and found several policemen pointing guns straight at him. He called out to them not to shoot, but they fired at him anyway and didn't miss.

The next stop was in Arabeh village at the home of Asel Asleh, a seventeen-year-old boy who had been active in dialogue between Arab and Jewish high school pupils. It's a middle-class home, well-appointed; both parents are professionals. Asel, everyone says, was a clean-cut kid, a good student, an outspoken peace activist; it is unimaginable that he was involved in violence. He did go to the demonstration, but he turned around to go home when the police arrived and things heated up. He was shot in the back of the neck. According to his father, eyewitnesses declare that they saw police officers perform a "kill confirmation": they shot him from close range after he was already down on the ground. Nevertheless, he was still alive, his spinal cord severed from his brain, when his father arrived on the scene. But police cordons delayed his evacuation to a hospital, and he died a few hours later. His mother says that, as a teacher, she's always tried to educate toward tolerance. But how can she do that now, after what's happened to her own son? The students won't take her seriously.

There are still a couple more things on my agenda. I drive over to pick up my son and a friend from their Jewish National Fund (JNF)-sponsored hiking club. The distance is walkable, but it's dark, and some of the rooms are nervous these days about letting kids walk around outside at night. Discussion in the car is about the hike scheduled for the Sukkot vacation, in a few days' time: will it take place, despite "the situation"?

Dangerous Roads

Finally, I get back into the car again to go to a study evening commemorating the thirtieth day of the passing of a good friend's mother-in-law, who died in the United States well before "the situation" began. My friend, Dafna (not her real name), lives in Gush Etzion. She invited me to this evening when I called her after Rosh Hashana to wish her a good new year and to hear from her at first hand about the hardships of living under siege.

There have been shootings almost daily at the main road leading to the Gush from Jerusalem—the same Jerusalem-Hebron highway that runs near my home. Just a few years ago, a new bypass, known as the "Tunnels Road," was built on the highway. It relies on a series of scenic bridges and tunnels blasted through the hills to take the road around rather than through the Arab towns and villages lining the old main road to Hebron via Bethlehem. The rationale was that this would make travel quicker and safer for residents of the Gush and also for residents of Jewish towns within the Green Line lying to the south of Jerusalem, accessible in pre-1967 terms only from the west. As a result, what used to be an hour's traveling time has been cut to fifteen minutes, and new bedroom suburbs have sprung up on both sides of the Green Line. In the transformed reality of "the situation," however, cars plying the bypass have become like ducks in an amusement-park shooting range, and the road is closed more often than not. In our phone conversation, Dafna asked me if she could camp out with her younger kids in our basement if war breaks out. "I'd rather watch it on television," she said, assuming that the war will stay there, twenty minutes' drive from my home.

But the commemorative evening is being held in one of Jerusalem's northern neighborhoods, so I have to drive nowhere more dramatic than the highway running along the "seam" between East and West Jerusalem. Traffic here is lighter than usual, since this road normally carries a lot of Arab traffic to and from Shuafat, Ramallah, and El Bireh, and those places are now blocked off. Though many of the participants in the study session are from the Gush, there's no settler rhetoric here. Many Gush residents are only moderately right wing, insisting on the national consensus that the area, which, according to the 1947 partition plan, was to have been part of the Jewish State, won't be "returned" to the Palestinians even under a peace agreement. The contents of this evening's study are some disconnected mishnayot [readings from the Talmud] about the rituals performed by the High Priest in the Temple on Yom Kippur. My thoughts wander briefly to the recent riots on the Temple Mount, but the political significance of the place, though the ground is burning under our feet, isn't part of the discussion.

Conflicting Points of View

Dafna and I don't see each other that often, and we snatch a few minutes to talk after the presentation is finished. Our conversation turns again to "the situation" and the difficulties being faced daily by the residents of the Gush. Dafna's eighteen-year-old daughter, who's studying in Jerusalem, is often stuck in town and can't get home. "Someone said to me that the situation now is as bad as 1948," Dafna tells me. I object: "In 1948 they had to bring water to Jerusalem under fire in tankers; it's not that bad just yet." Still thinking of my spouse's experiences earlier that day, I point out that as hard as it is in the Gush, it's even worse for the Arabs. But they started the violence in the first place, Dafna protests. I tell her about Asel, shot in the back of the neck; Asel's mother is mourning a dead child. "But what was he doing at that demonstration in the first place?" Dafna demands, refusing to sympathize. "I go to demonstrations, too," I reply, "and I don't expect to be shot in the head." We drop the subject and exchange notes on our sons' forthcoming bar mitzvahs instead. I walk out with Dafna as the men in the party exchange stern remarks about what route to use to drive home. The Tunnels Road is closed again; they'll have to drive the long way around, via Beit Shemesh. Someone calls his wife to tell her he'll be home late.

I get into my car and drive back through the lower-class Shmuel HaNavi neighborhood, part Mizrahi and part ultra-Orthodox, and on through ultra-Orthodox Geula. People are preparing for Sukkot, lugging planks and palm fronds through the streets, seemingly unconcerned about the traffic, though these are main roads with bus routes. I'm driving slowly, but I have to jam on the brakes twice to avoid hitting pedestrians who walk in front of my car. I arrive home almost shaking. The hour is late now, but Yael, a neighbor whose politics are similar to mine, is out walking her dog. "The whole country's gone crazy," I blurt out to her. "The Jews, the Arabs, the settlers, probably me, too, at least in the eyes of someone else." I tell her I feel like a character in the story by Rabbi Nachman of Bratzlav about the master and his servant who saw everyone around them being struck with madness. Knowing that the same fate would surely befall them as well, they put marks on their foreheads to remind each other that they were not sane. Yael is sympathetic. She is a former German Christian who converted to Judaism because she found it the best way to repudiate the Nazi past. Here, in Jerusalem, she works tirelessly to explain the Holocaust to non-Jews and to resist the oppression of the Palestinians.

Fighting for Space

I finally go to bed. In the morning I reach for the newspaper, and a small headline catches my eye: two men from the settlement of Eli who were with Alon when he was run over have been arrested. By their own admission, they were out on the road the previous morning stoning Arab cars. The real reason we buried Kokhi's brother is that the Arab driver lost control of his car after being hit by a rock.

One more epilogue: Later that day I visit Kokhi, who's sitting shiva for her brother at her parents' home on Hebron Road. A half-hour drive northward across town, up the continuation of the same road, would bring me to Ramallah, where the lynching has now happened and Israeli combat helicopters have just finished their reprisal bombing. Jerusalem's hilly terrain prevents us from hearing the blasts. With the Tunnels Road closed and little commuter traffic, it's eerily quiet in what should be the evening rush hour.

Though it's only a few minutes' walk from my own home, the house where Kokhi grew up is in a different world. My family's apartment, far from luxurious, is in a pleasant, middle-class neighborhood, surrounded by tall trees. Kokhi's parents' place is a tiny top-floor walk-up in one of the slummy blocks that line Hebron Road on its way out of town, built in the 1950s to get new immigrants from the Middle East and North Africa out of transit camps. The place is packed, mostly with men listening to a talk being given by the rabbi between the afternoon and evening prayers; some women, mostly hatted, are sitting in the two small back rooms. Squeezing myself in, I find Kokhi in a t-shirt in the kitchen, which is piled high with food brought in for a large family sitting shiva. There's barely room for both of us to stand, but we exchange a few words. I ask her how many brothers and sisters they were. "Seven, before," she replies sadly. I look around and cannot imagine a family of nine living and growing in such a small space, and then I think of Alon, whom I never met, looking for a place where he could raise his family comfortably. Cheap land, cheap housing, has been available for years in the territories, which is one reason Dafna is out there, too. The conflict between Arabs and Jews in the Land of Israel/Palestine isn't only a matter of passion, ethnicity, or religion; it is a battle for space, living space, a battle forced by economic reality as much as anything else.

I press Kokhi's hand and go out into the night, back home, where my kids are waiting for me to buy string to put up our Sukkot decorations.

A Palestinian Refugee Visits His Home

John Donnelly

When Israel won its independence in 1948, many Palestinians who fled their homes during the fighting were never allowed by the Israeli government to return, despite a 1949 resolution by the United Nations that declared the right of the refugees to return to their homes. John Donnelly, a staff writer for the *Boston Globe*, recounts the story of one of these refugees in the following article. According to Donnelly, Ahmed Salem al-Masri, a Palestinian farmer, fled his home village of Ajjur with his wife and children during the war in 1948. Al-Masri now lives in the Deheishe refugee camp, the author writes, and has only been able to visit the site of his native village a few times in the past fifty years. Donnelly accompanies al-Masri to the fields and olive groves that he once owned, bearing witness to the old man's joy at seeing his land again and his grief over what he has lost.

The old man greeted his tree softly and bent his stiff frame. He kissed the gnarled tree trunk and rested his forehead upon it. His tears fell to the tree's feet.

"Hello, my olive tree," he said.

For just the third time in 50 years, Ahmed Salem al-Masri, 83, was standing on what once had been his land in Ajjur, Palestine, a place that hasn't existed since 1948.

He was in Israel now. For nearly all of those 50 years, al-Masri's olive grove has belonged to someone else, untended, unharvested, and surrounded by six strands of barbed wire. Ajjur, once a sprawling village, is now home to five small Jewish towns, fields with modern irrigation equipment and two Israeli nature reserves.

Al-Masri left the olive tree and kissed another, patting it as he would an old friend. His step suddenly had spring. He slipped through an opening in a stone wall, walked quickly across a field, passed another stone wall as if it weren't there, and headed toward an olive grove.

John Donnelly, "Palestinians Who Have Suffered Since 1948 Rarely Recognized," *Knight-Ridder/Tribune News Service*, April 2, 1998, p. 402K7067. Copyright © 1998 by *Knight-Ridder/Tribune News Service*. Reproduced by permission.

Over his shoulder, he said, "I feel as if I was born again."

Al-Masri is one of 600,000 to 700,000 Palestinians who lost their lands and homes in 1948. Ajjur is one of 350 to 450 Arab villages destroyed by Jewish soldiers during the first Israel-Arab war, which Israelis call their War of Independence and Palestinians call "Nakhbah," which is Arabic for catastrophe.

Those who have turned to violence and terrorism in an effort to avenge the catastrophe or retake their old lands have captured the headlines. Those such as al-Masri who have suffered in silence have remained largely invisible.

The Losers of 1948

Israel's 50th birthday gala in Jerusalem on April 30, 1998, which will be attended by luminaries from around the world, with Vice President Al Gore heading the U.S. delegation, will focus on the country's storied accomplishments. In this hard land, the Israelis have built a modern democratic state, rebuilt a national identity and revived the Hebrew language. They will celebrate the ingathering of Jews after 2,000 years of exile, the creation of the Middle East's most powerful military force, and the can-do spirit of its new high-tech economic engine.

They will not mention the losers of 1948, the Palestinians.

About the only Israeli reflection on the Palestinians' plight has come in a television documentary called *Tekuma*, which produced two out of 22 segments from the Arab perspective. The subject matter was so sensitive that the show's host quit in protest and Israel's communications minister demanded the cancellation of the entire series because of the episodes on the Palestinians. Nevertheless, the show has gone on.

The Arab nations that today are home to more than 3.5 million Palestinians have used the Palestinians' cause as a rallying cry against Israel, but they also have left three generations of Palestinians to fend for themselves in miserable refugee camps on the outskirts of Amman, Beirut and Damascus.

At the negotiating table in the comatose Israeli-Palestinian peace talks, the unfinished business of 1948 has been pushed to a far corner where it is gathering dust. The negotiations now are about whether Israel will give back more of the West Bank, which was captured from Jordan after Arab armies attacked Israel in 1967.

Even Yasser Arafat's Palestinian Authority does not devote much more than lip service to the losers of 1948. Palestinian cultural and religious groups in the West Bank and Gaza are hosting conferences and talks about the "Nakhbah," but so far the lectures have been sparsely attended.

"We don't need a big Hollywood production," said Adila Laidi, director of the Khalil Sakakini Cultural Center in the West Bank town of Ramallah, which is sponsoring a series of 15 talks by witnesses of the battles and the Palestinian exodus a half-century ago. "Our story stands on its own."

The Birth of Israel

The story, told in dramatically different ways depending on one's politics, has filled books.

On May 15, 1948, Jewish leaders declared the birth of the state of Israel from an auditorium in Tel Aviv. Hours later, the tiny new nation's Arab neighbors bombed the city and launched a multi-pronged attack. Months of fighting followed, and the Israelis piled up a string of victories.

Over several months, hundreds of thousands of Palestinians fled, finding their way to Egypt's Gaza Strip, to Jordan's West Bank and to points beyond—to other parts of Jordan and Egypt, and to Syria, Lebanon, the Gulf states, Europe, and the United States.

Over the next three years, 546,000 Jewish immigrants flooded the new state, nearly doubling Israel's population. At the same time, several hundred thousand Palestinians flooded United Nations refugee camps, which at first were little more than tent cities.

Although in 1949 the U.N. passed Resolution 194, which says the Palestinian refugees have an "inalienable right" to return to their homes in what is now Israel, the camps remain home to a third generation of Palestinians. The camps will remain, U.N. officials say, until the issue is resolved.

For all the legalistic wrangling and political posturing, the issue was resolved long ago. The Israelis won and the Palestinians lost. While Israelis watch birthday fireworks, Palestinians will be closing their shutters.

"For Palestinians, the 50th anniversary of Israel is a reminder of their anguish. It scratches their wounds," said Hisham Ahmed, an American-educated political scientist who grew up in the Deheishe camp near al-Masri's home.

But, he added: "It doesn't mean it's forgotten. No, never. It remains always in the minds of people who lived through it. In people's minds, this is Palestinian land."

A Palestinian Refugee's Story

Ahmed Salem al-Masri daydreams about Ajjur every day. It is 19 miles and one Israeli army checkpoint from his home in the refugee camp at Deheishe.

In deference to his wisdom, everyone calls al-Masri "the Haj," after the pilgrimage to Mecca every Muslim should make at least once in his life. He never attended school. His father died when he was two years old, and when he was a boy his family depended upon him to watch over the livestock. From the age of five, he knew each olive tree and each cow that belonged to his family.

"We were peasants," he recalled in his family's living room. "We had cattle, cows, sheep, camels. Our houses were full of all sorts of goods. From wheat to parsley, all from our earth. We were living like kings on our lands."

When he was 23, al-Masri married Jamila, who was six years younger. As was the custom, he asked her family for her hand and won their approval. They wed, and talked to each other for the first time that night.

In Ajjur, Ahmed and Jamila al-Masri had two children—two others died after childbirth. Their lives were married to the seasons. "In September, we would till the soil," said Ahmed. "The rains would come and two or three months later we would till the soil again. We would pick the olives when the season came. In the summer, we would take a little time off and relax until September, when we were back farming again."

Most days, al-Masri awoke at 3:30 A.M., ate breakfast and was in his fields by 4 A.M. At mid-morning, Jamila would bring him bread, butter and yogurt, all made on their farm. In hot weather, he napped in the afternoons and then returned to the fields until 9 P.M.

"I loved summers," he said, smiling at the memory. "It was the season when you had all the fruits and vegetables. We had wheat, barley, lentils, chick peas, corn, olives, grapes, figs, apricots, beans, tomatoes, everything. We were self-sufficient. We had all we needed."

Ajjur's Muslim roots are believed to date back to the early years of the Fatamids, between 909 and 1171, according to *All That Remains*, an encyclopedia published by the Institute for Palestine Studies in Washington on Palestinian villages that were destroyed in the 1948 war.

Just before the war, the village of 3,730 people, 566 houses, two schools and two mosques was almost entirely pastoral. Some 48 percent of the land was cultivated with wheat and olives.

Then came war. About 400 local men and some 400 Egyptian troops defended Ajjur, which was supposed to be part of a new Palestinian state according to a United Nations plan for partitioning British-ruled Palestine into a Jewish and an Arab state.

Al-Masri was in the local militia. Israeli soldiers attacked twice in the late summer of 1948, but the Egyptians and locals held the village. On Oct. 7, the Egyptians left town.

Fleeing from Home

On the morning of Oct. 10, al-Masri, fearing a new attack, carried a sack of wheat to a cave a mile and a half from his home where he kept his cattle. Returning, he saw Jamila coming toward him. "She was carrying the baby, dragging the other child and balancing a basket with four or five chickens in it."

He asked: "Where are you going? What has happened?"

She replied: "We had to leave, there was a rain of bullets on our house."

They walked back to the cave and later hired a truck to take them to Hebron.

As part of Operative Yo'av, the 4th Battalion of the Israeli army's Givati Brigade occupied Ajjur, according to the official *History of the War of Independence*. According to that account, the capture of Ajjur enabled the Givati Brigade to join Israel's southern and central flanks in the Hebron District.

Al-Masri and his family began new lives as refugees. They moved from place to place, staying for awhile in the village of Beit Sahour near Bethlehem and eventually moving into the Deheishe refugee camp.

There they lived a miserable existence for many years. In the mid-1950s, the U.N. built one room per family. People dug holes in back-yards to dump their waste. They took water from shared pipes. House-holds didn't hook up to Bethlehem's electric grid until the late 1970s.

The al-Masris had four more children, and Ahmed found a succession of odd jobs. Several times, he farmed someone else's land in Jordan. Once, in 1974, he returned to his former land to pick olives. The new landowners, Israelis, allowed Palestinians to pick the crop and keep a portion of it.

Al-Masri was picking olives with a dozen Palestinian women when a rabbi approached the group.

"Someone had told him that the land belonged to me," al-Masri said. "The rabbi walked up to me and said the land now belonged to the Israeli government." Al-Masri said nothing. He left soon after.

A Chance to Return

In 1978, he had a second chance to return. He landed a well-paying job with an Israeli security company that assigned guards to watch heavy equipment that was being used to build new homes for Israeli residents.

"Ironically," al-Masri said, "I watched bulldozers in the hills of Ajjur."

For several months, he camped out in his old village, not far from what had been his land.

"I had a weird feeling," he said. "I loved being there but my conscience was torn. On one hand, I had a personal responsibility to protect the equipment. On the other hand, I felt all along something should be done to stop the building."

The nights were the most difficult. "Those were the hours of thinking, anticipating, wondering," he remembers. "At one point, I said to myself, 'How crazy is it to come to your land that is stolen from you to watch the machines of your enemy.' But I had to balance that with wanting to support my family. I would stay awake nights asking God to do something to the people who stole my land."

His job ended abruptly. "One day a Jewish man came to me and asked where I was from. I said Ajjur. I started crying. He asked again, 'Whose land is this? Yours? This is untrue.'

"I felt as if I had slapped him on the face. I didn't mean to provoke any problems. I didn't mean that I wanted to take over the land. I just stated the fact.

"The man came back with my employer and the man told him, 'Get him out of here.'"

His employer reassigned al-Masri to another site.

Almost 50 years after he left Ajjur, al-Masri showed a visitor his backyard garden in the Deheishe refugee camp, among the crumbling concrete buildings and swarms of neighborhood children. The garden didn't look like much, just an olive tree, a tree that grows the sweet yellow lowquat fruit, some grapevines and a few rows of vegetables. But to him, it was his old garden in miniature.

"It brings me back there," he said, his chest rattling as he took a breath.

Asked if he would return to his old home, he didn't hesitate. "I would love to go to Ajjur," he said.

On the next morning he went, riding in silence almost the entire time.

Coming Home Again

It took al-Masri a few minutes to find the site of his old house. That was mostly because a new road, Route 353, ran over it. He found the site only by locating a fig tree and some cactus plants that had rimmed his property.

He said his land was atop a nearby hill, about 500 yards down the road, and he wanted to see it. Stepping through an opening in the barbed wire fence, al-Masri hesitated. "Please, God, help me," he whispered.

The old man walked slowly, stooping every so often to pick wild plants. First, he pulled up marou, a green bulb-like plant that tastes like honey. Then he found a huge clump of zatar, prized in the Middle East and elsewhere for its medicinal qualities.

Finally, he reached the southern edge of his old property. He sat on a large rock. "This is the rock I used to sit on," he said.

He moved on to his old land, kissed the first olive tree and kept walking until he had seen nearly all 26 acres. Then he finally rested.

"This land used to be healthy, but look at it now. It's all ruins," he said. "How are the Palestinians going to come back here? The Israelis won't give it away. They are like a dog who grabbed a bone and will never let go."

The "Haj" told a long story about how his great-grandfather's first wife had fallen in a well and died. He told of how his great-grandfather had spent three days in a well after refusing to pay taxes, how he had found a second wife in Egypt and how he had planted more olive trees to mark his land and make sure no one stole it.

He laughed at the stories, then fell silent.

After several minutes, he stood. "We can go down now," he said. "What a waste it is not be here to till the soil."

He walked to his olive tree.

"Goodbye, my olive tree," he whispered, his hands holding the gnarled trunk. "Who knows whether we will see each other again?"

CHAPTER 4

PROPOSALS FOR
CREATING PEACE
BETWEEN ISRAEL
AND PALESTINE

Contemporary Issues
Companion

OVERCOMING THE OBSTACLES TO PEACE

Cherie R. Brown

According to Cherie R. Brown, there are four major obstacles to Jewish participation in the peace process. Misinformation about the true causes of problems in the peace negotiations, the legacy of the Holocaust, feelings of isolation from the global community, and a political generation gap combine to prevent many Jewish people from believing peace is possible, she writes. Brown proposes eight principles that she maintains can help Jews in Israel and elsewhere to organize for peace in the Middle East. These principles include acknowledging that both Israelis and Palestinians have the right to exist, that both sides have been hurt, and that continued violence by either side is not the answer to the conflict. By embracing the principles for peace, Brown contends, Jews can work successfully to bring the current impasse in the peace process to an end. Brown is the director of the National Coalition Building Institute in Washington, D.C.

I have been working primarily with U.S. Jews since 1967 on behalf of a just solution to the Arab-Israeli conflict. Before we can organize Jews on behalf of peace, we need to recognize four obstacles to Jewish participation in the peace process. Once we face these four obstacles, we can build on eight simple principles I offer here as the basis for renewing hope in a new Middle East peace initiative.

Four Obstacles to Peace

Obstacle #1: There is still a great deal of misinformation about the real causes of the most recent breakdown in peace efforts. This misinformation has left Jews feeling hopeless and susceptible to increased mistrust of Palestinians.

Most Jews (and a large majority of the U.S. press) were led to believe that [Israeli prime minister] Ehud Barak had made a generous offer to the Palestinian people in 2000 and that the blame therefore was primarily with Yasser Arafat and the Palestinian leadership for not accepting such a good offer. Many Jews were never given the real facts "on the ground"—that this "generous" offer meant that Palestinians were permanently saddled with Israeli military roadblocks and checkpoints throughout Palestinian occupied land. In addition, there were no arrangements in the settlement for any compensation or even any discussion of Palestinian refugee issues. When this peace offer was rejected, many Jews decided that there was no hope for real cooperation with Palestinians. This loss of hope has been a major roadblock to reaching out to Jews and to engaging them in renewed efforts for peace.

Obstacle #2: Given the history of the Holocaust and the attempted genocide of Jews, it has been extremely difficult for many Jews to be able to see ourselves in the oppressor role with regards to another people.

I recently watched an excellent new film by an Israeli film maker— *The Promise*—which showed a group of young Palestinian children and young Israeli children being brought together over a two-year trust-building period. In the film, a number of hard-hitting scenes were shown about daily life for Palestinians under the Occupation, including being stopped at military checkpoints throughout the occupied territories. As I watched these scenes, I found myself hardly breathing. I wanted to scream out, "It can't be this bad. Are you sure this is balanced enough? Please don't show this picture of Israel to the world. They will just end up hating the Israeli people!" While my mind knew this was a true picture of Palestinian life under occupation—and needed to be known—my heart rebelled. I have been working for justice for Palestinians for thirty years, and I could hardly watch these scenes. And these are not the most hard-hitting scenes of Palestinian life under occupation. We are going to need to find a way to make it safe enough for Jews to remember how good we are so we are able to take an honest look at the oppressor role that Israel has been set up to play with the Palestinian people. Jews will not be able to face the oppressive things that the Israeli government does unless we know that the world still believes we are a deeply good people.

Obstacle #3: Jews continue to feel isolated and unable to reach out for allies out of a sense of terror and powerlessness.

I attended the nongovernmental organizations (NGO) meeting of the United Nations Conference on Racism in August 2001 in Durban, South Africa. It was, at times, a painful place to be as a Jew. Israel was unfairly singled out for condemnation in several of the proposed documents and sessions at the conference. At one point during the week, the Jewish Caucus made up T-shirts with a Jewish star and a peace symbol on the front and a quote from Martin Luther King, Jr. on the back. As I walked from tent to tent at the conference, I saw groups of Jewish young people, wearing their T-shirts, huddled together with each other for support. The attacks on Israel had left these young Jews feeling vulnerable and isolated. They weren't able to reach out and build friendships with other anti-racist activists from around the world. And without these friendships, it was impossible to have allies who could stand up both for Israel and for the Palestinian people. I understood in Durban, in a whole new way, how difficult it was, even for some of my closest friends, to stand up fully for Palestinians and not feel like they were somehow betraying Jews—or to stand up fully against the singling out of Israel for condemnation and not to feel like they were somehow betraying the Palestinian people. And this is what is needed—allies who will stand up clearly for both peoples no matter how much pressure there is to take sides.

Obstacle #4: There is a generation gap between progressive Jews who were born before 1967 and those who were born after the annexation of the West Bank and Gaza that is hindering the building of an effective Jewish peace coalition.

Progressive Jews who were born prior to 1967 (some who lived through World War II, others who know that there was no place for Jewish refugees to go after the war) often say in their organizing efforts that they are speaking out against the policies of the Israeli government out of a deep love of Israel and an understanding of the need for Israel as a necessary homeland for the Jewish people. Those who were born after 1967—when the Occupation was firmly in place—have little collective memory of World War II or of Jews as victims. Therefore, they often focus their efforts on ending the Occupation and the oppressive policies of the Israeli government but do not always add that their organizing efforts are based in a love of Israel or a need for a homeland for the Jewish people. Each group is going to need to be listened to fully and this "generational rift" healed if an effective new Jewish progressive peace coalition is to be built in this next period. A love of Israel (the older generation's key concern)—which is then linked to the end of the Occupation (the younger generation's key concern)—needs to be foremost in any new Middle East peace project that we set up.

Eight Principles for Peace

How are we going to break through these obstacles and develop a new Middle East peace project? I would like to propose eight simple working principles about human beings that could form the basis of a new Middle East peace effort. These working principles are based on an understanding that what is needed now to break the current impasse is not one more analysis of the conflict (God knows—we have enough people fighting to have us agree with their analysis and perspective), but instead a simple set of guidelines about what is true about Jews and Palestinians that will give us enough hope to keep moving forward.

Principle #1: It is no longer possible to destroy the State of Israel or the Palestinian people—and their right to justice and statehood. Both peoples have too many allies worldwide. Both peoples exist and both peoples will continue to exist. The attempted destruction of any people weakens the struggle for liberation of everyone.

Principle #2: There *is* a just solution for all involved in the Palestinian-Israeli conflict and we are capable of finding it—including on the issue of Jerusalem. It must be recognized that Israel cannot have lasting peace without an economically viable nation for the Palestinian people.

Principle #3: Both sides do hurtful things and both sides have been hurt. Given the injustices that both peoples have faced, each group is going to need to be listened to far more than they have been to date. The small number of listening projects that have been organized have been important, but more resources will need to be put into expanding these listening projects in this next period.

Principle #4: There are no human enemies. Both sides have and will behave irrationally in response to having been hurt. We will never be able to undue or redress all the past mistreatment. However, when both sides have been listened to fully (Principle #3), each will be more able to think clearly about solutions. Solutions to the conflict will need to be based primarily on what will work in the present.

Principle #5: There is reason for continued hope in the present situation. What appears to be a difficult moment is, in reality, a time when the unresolved difficulties can come to the surface for further understanding. For example, the latest round of violence demonstrated that the recent peace talks did not have the clear backing of large segments of the Palestinian population or significant segments of the Israeli population. The backing of large enough portions of both populations will be necessary for any final peace settlement. The recent difficulties are providing new opportunities that, if taken, could lead to more effective solutions. And this is very hopeful.

Principle #6: None of the violence that has happened in the recent period negates any of the important and useful efforts towards cooperation that have taken place in the past. Every cooperative effort from the past has been important, no matter how much these efforts have been covered over by discouragement.

Principle #7: It does not make sense to call for an end to Palestinian violence without also calling for an end to Israeli military domination of Palestinians. The domination of one people by another—no matter how much that domination is based in a real perceived fear—will not result in an end to violence.

Principle #8: Real solutions will come when we apply our thinking to the actual issues and struggles in the present as distinct from the painful emotion that surrounds these issues and struggles. Painful emotion needs to be listened to but it should not be the basis for formulating policy.

Restoring Hope

The obstacles to organizing Jews on behalf of a just peace in the Middle East can seem overwhelming at times. But they are not insurmountable. Every impasse in the past has eventually given way to the next steps in the negotiation process. This period is no different. This impasse will end. And all of our continued efforts, including these eight proposed principles, will enable us to move past the current paralysis and restore hope in a permanent and just peace.

ISRAEL MUST ABANDON ITS CLAIM OF BEING A JEWISH HOMELAND

Allan C. Brownfeld

The Israeli government actively encourages the immigration of all Jewish people to Israel, writes Allan C. Brownfeld, the editor of *Issues*, the quarterly journal of the American Council for Judaism. According to Brownfeld, Israel considers itself the Jewish homeland and insists that a true Jewish life can only be lived within its borders. However, Brownfeld points out, this idea has contributed to the continuation of the territorial conflict between Israel and the Palestinians. Israel is unable to withdraw from the occupied territories and accept the formation of a Palestinian state because it believes this land is necessary for the settlement of Jews from around the world, he maintains. But this concept has a significant flaw, Brownfeld argues: Far from considering themselves to be exiles, most Jewish people living in other countries are happy to remain where they are. Only when the Israeli government acknowledges that the nation should be a home for all its citizens—not just Jews—can a lasting peace be achieved, Brownfeld concludes.

As the world—and U.S. policymakers—focus upon the continuing Israeli-Palestinian impasse, it is important to examine a serious stumbling block along the path to any lasting settlement which has been long ignored. That is Israel's continuing claim to be the "homeland" not only of its own citizens—but of Jews throughout the world. It is, after all, to make room for the hoped-for emigration to Israel of millions of Jews who are citizens of other countries that there is an unwillingness to withdraw from the occupied territories and compromise in accepting the reality of a Palestinian state.

For many years, the State of Israel and the adherents of Zionism in other countries have maintained the position that Israel is the "Jewish homeland," that Jews outside of Israel are in "exile," and that a "full Jewish life" can be lived only in the Jewish state. In our own country, even the leaders of Reform Judaism recently adopted a statement of

Allan C. Brownfeld, "For Lasting Peace, Israel Must Be Content to Be a Homeland for All Its Citizens—Not All Jews," *Washington Report on Middle East Affairs*, vol. 21, March 2002, p. 71. Copyright © 2002 by American Educational Trust. Reproduced by permission.

principles holding that Israel is "central" to Jewish life and encouraging *aliyah*, or emigration to Israel.

Israel as the Center of Jewish Life

On a visit to Germany in 1996, Israeli President Ezer Weizman declared that he "cannot understand how 40,000 Jews can live in Germany" and asserted that, "The place of Jews is in Israel. Only in Israel can Jews live full Jewish lives."

In 1998, Israeli Prime Minister Binyamin Netanyahu called upon American Jews to make a "mass *aliyah*" to Israel. The head of the Jewish Agency, Avram Burg, declared that the synagogue in Western countries is the "symbol of destruction," and that the new center of Jewish life should be the state of Israel.

In 2000, Israeli President Moshe Katsev called upon Jews throughout the world to make *aliyah* and argued against "legitimizing" Jewish life in other countries. In a book published in 2000, *Conversations with Yitzhak Shamir*, the former Israeli prime minister declared: "The very essence of our being obliges every Jew to live in Eretz Yisrael. . . . In my opinion, a man has no right to consider himself a part of the Jewish People without also being a Zionist, because Zionism states that in order for a Jew to live as a Jew he needs to have his own country, his own life, and his own future."

It can be said that Israel's abnormality began with its declaration on May 15, 1948 that it was a state not of the people living within its borders, but of the "Jewish people" everywhere. The Law of Return, which gave Jews the right to emigration and citizenship, codified this "Jewish people" concept when it held that, "The State of Israel considers itself as the creation of the Jewish people," and endowed every Jew with the right to permanent settlement. David Ben-Gurion declared in 1952 that, "The State of Israel is a part of the Middle East only in geography, which is, in the main, a static element. From the more decisive standpoint of dynamism, creation and growth, Israel is a part of world Jewry."

The Israeli High Court in January 1972 declared: "There is no Israeli nation apart from the Jewish people residing in Israel and in the diaspora." Clearly, if Jews outside were to be considered part of the state and were to be "ingathered," room had to be made for them.

Calling Jews to Israel

In her book *The Fate of the Jews*, Roberta Strauss Feurlicht notes that ". . . the Zionists chose to create a state by superseding the indigenous population and culture of Palestine and ingathering from all over the world descendants of Jews who had not lived there in any number for 2,000 years and who no longer shared language or culture or anything else except the identification 'Jewish'. . . . Zionism has always been a minority position among Jews and remains so; otherwise, there would not be so many Jews unsettling in Israel."

In 1917, at the time of the Balfour Declaration, Jews were only 10 percent of the population of Palestine. By 1946, Jews were still only 31 percent of the population Moshe Dayan once declared: "We came to this country that was already populated by Arabs, and we are establishing a Hebrew, that is a Jewish state here. . . . Jewish villages were built in the place of Arab villages. . . . There is not one place built in this country that did not have a former Arab population."

The attitude of many Zionists was expressed by Joseph Weitz when he headed the Jewish National Fund: "It must be clear that there is no room for both peoples in this country. . . . There is no room for compromise on this point! . . . We must not leave a single village, not a single tribe."

Israel's prime minister, Ariel Sharon, has called repeatedly upon American Jews—and Jews in other countries—to emigrate to Israel. During the battle over the Falkland Islands, Sharon said that British and Argentinean Jews were in a war "that does not belong to them."

The fact is that the vast majority of Jews throughout the world reject the idea that they are in "exile" and that Israel is their real "homeland."

While Jewish organizations in the U.S. place Israel at the "center" of their agenda, for American Jews Israel remains a largely peripheral interest.

Israel Is a Peripheral Interest

In their study *The Jew Within: Self, Family and Community in America*, authors Steven M. Cohen, associate professor at the Melton School for Jewish Education at the Hebrew University in Jerusalem, and Arnold M. Eisen, professor of religious studies at Stanford University, explored the foundations of belief and behavior among moderately affiliated American Jews.

The authors report that, "Their connection to Israel . . . is weak, as is the connection to the organized Jewish community in America. They take for granted the compatibility of being both Jewish and American; this is simply not an issue anymore. . . . They want to be Jewish because of what it means to them personally—not because of obligation to the Jewish group . . . or the historical destiny of the Jewish group."

When asked about their emotional attachment to Israel, just 9 percent of respondents answered "extremely attached." Professors Cohen and Eisen stress that, "It is no longer uncommon to find lukewarm-to-cool attitudes to Israel coexisting with warm-to-passionate feelings about being Jewish. . . . Israel is not central to who American Jews are as Jews—and so the need to visit it, or learn about it, or wrestle with its importance for the Jewish people is far from pressing."

Indeed, if there are some Jews who view their homes in the U.S., or

England or France or Argentina, as "diaspora" and "exile," they are a small but vocal minority. In his book, *Home Lands: Portraits of the New Jewish Diaspora*, Larry Tye shows that Israel is clearly not the only place in which Jews can fully live their faith, and is not viewed by most Jews in the world as, somehow, their genuine "homeland." Beyond this, he urges that the very term "diaspora" be eliminated.

Jews Are Not Exiles

The word "diaspora," writes Tye, a reporter for the *Boston Globe*, "suggests an existence as unsettled as it is unsatisfying. It describes a homogeneous people uprooted and dispersed from their native land by unstoppable armies or irreversible social forces. It bespeaks a yearning to go back. The Irish know all about having to abandon their homeland and the loss it creates. So do Armenians and Chinese, Kurds and Kosovars. But the oldest diaspora is that of the Jews. It dates back at least 1,900 years, to when Rome toppled the Second Temple in Jerusalem and Jews were scattered across Asia, Africa and Europe. Each time they settled somewhere new, a new persecutor—the inquisitors of Spain, the Russian czars, Hitler and the Holocaust he unleashed—reminded them that they were strangers, with the perils that implied. For . . . millennia, Jews have vowed to make their community whole again by returning to their homeland, the Holy Land. Each year at Passover Seder, parents and children end by reciting a solemn vow, 'Next year in Jerusalem!'"

Tye points out that while "the metaphor of a people longing to go home is compelling," in today's world "it is also outdated."

Jerusalem, he says, is an idea, not an address, a metaphor for the day the world lives in spiritual and earthly peace—not a destination for today's Jews who are, he finds, very much at home in the various nations of the world.

At Home Around the World

In this book, Tye explores Jewish communities in seven cities on four continents. He found that Jews are more likely to base their identity on their own spiritual experience, not on the religious institutions of the past or the Zionist concept of a separate Jewish nationalism.

The idea that "diaspora Jews are residing in some unnatural exile," Tye declares, "is a distortion of history. The First and Second Temples, and the golden ages they represented, were relative brief notations on a Jewish time line that is, instead, dominated by diaspora. Abraham, father of the Jews, discovered his God outside Israel. The Torah was given to the Jewish people outside Israel. The most important Talmud, or compilation of Jewish traditions, is the one from Babylon, not the one from Jerusalem. Even during the era of the Second Temple, more Jews lived in the diaspora than in Israel. 'Displacement,' then, has been the normal state of affairs for Jews for nearly 2,600 years."

Focusing on Buenos Aires, Dusseldorf, Paris, Dublin, Boston, Atlanta and the Ukrainian city of Dnepropetrovsk, Tye notes that, "The more communities I got to see close-up, the clearer it became that the Jewish world was being revitalized and reshaped in many ways that . . . were not reflected in all the books I was reading about the disappearing diaspora and the vanishing Jews of America."

The place of Israel in Jewish life is far different from the myths which have been created about it, in Tye's view: "The founding of Israel half a century ago seemed to answer what Jews of the diaspora were longing for. Now, at last, they had a place of their own to go to, a way to end their physical isolation and realize the promise of celebrating a Seder in Jerusalem. That is a potent image, and for more than 50 years its promise and seduction have held the collective Jewish subconscious in a powerful grip. But like many metaphors this one does not fit the real-life aspirations and situations of most diaspora Jews today. It is wonderful to know that there is, finally, a homeland that would welcome us. Yet most of us have finally built secure lives . . . and have no interest in adjusting to the strange climate and society of Israel. Indeed, the busiest traffic today between Israel and the biggest diaspora county, America, could be called *aliyah* in reverse, with four times as many Israelis living in America as U.S. Jews living in Israel."

The Freedom to Live Only in Israel

When the former Soviet Union finally opened its door to allow Jewish emigration, Israel was outraged that the majority of Russian Jews preferred other destinations. Israel attempted to force thousands of Jews to resettle there rather than in the U.S. by requiring them to travel through Romania to take direct flights to Jerusalem. The Reagan administration regarded this Israeli effort as violating freedom of choice in emigration. In the end, it failed.

Similarly, Germany's decision to welcome Russian Jewish immigrants was vigorously opposed by Israel. In the early 1990s, senior Israeli officials told then-Chancellor Kohl to stop taking in Russian Jews who "belong" to Israel. Burkhard Hirsch, former vice president of the Bundestag, recalls that, "I met several times during visits to Jerusalem with high-ranking political groups who said, 'Why do you let Jews from Russia immigrate to Germany? We need them in Israel.' Our answer was, 'What is our right to tell them where they have to live?'"

In one of his first statements as prime minister in March 2001 Ariel Sharon called for Israel to continue aggressively recruiting diaspora Jews and said Israel is "the only place in the world where Jews can continue to live as Jews and withstand the danger of assimilation."

Even most Israelis, Larry Tye found, "think otherwise . . . they acknowledged that Jews can live rewarding Jewish lives in places like New York, Paris, and even Dusseldorf."

Roberta Strauss Feuerlicht declared that, "Zionism has disproved itself, or rather, Israel has disproved Zionism. Zionism was supposed to mean an in-gathering of the exiles, but Jews are not settling in Israel because political Zionism is too negative for them and spiritual Zionism is beyond their reach. Besides, most Jews are content to stay where they are. Life is not always better for Jews in Israel . . . often it is markedly worse. . . . Israel has always feared it would become a Levantine state, but ancient Israel was a Levantine state, and modern Israel will be accepted by its neighbors only when it accepts the fact that it must face east, not west."

It is essential for a genuine peace agreement that Israel abandons its concept of limitless nationality. The space required for the fanciful notion of an "ingathering" of those who do not believe they are in "exile" represents a threat of expansion and explains the unwillingness to compromise over the West Bank, Jerusalem, and the Gaza Strip. Those who are genuinely concerned with Israel's security and long-term well being should help it to understand this reality.

GIVING UP LAND WILL NOT CREATE PEACE

Colin Leci

In the following selection, political commentator and Middle East expert Colin Leci argues that withdrawing Israeli occupation from Palestinian territories will not solve the Arab-Israeli conflict. Promoters of the "land for peace" policy should consider that the Jewish people have been giving up their land in exchange for peace since World War I, he contends, while the Arabs have yet to respond in kind by relinquishing some of their territory to Israel. Furthermore, he insists, in the past Israel conceded land that it should have kept in order to maintain national security. Many Israelis were wounded or killed in Palestinian attacks before the Israeli occupation of the West Bank and the Gaza Strip began in 1967, Leci asserts, and ending the occupation will only expose the Israeli people to even more terror and violence. Israel must not give up more land at the expense of its security and independence, the author concludes.

The time has come for all those who believe in the Land for Peace ideal to face reality and reflect on the situation prior to 1967. During the period between 1948 and 1967, the tortuous and elongated border between Israel and its neighbors was annually the scene of hundreds of Arab raids across the line. Israeli men, women, and children were killed indiscriminately, villages were attacked, houses blown up, and civilians kidnapped in unending Arab guerrilla warfare. It is possible, of course, that those who subscribed to the policy of land for peace, including Prime Minister Barak, had either forgotten or possibly were not even born when these civil incidents took place and felt that by giving land for peace, the situation that occurred in the 19-odd years from 1948 would not repeat itself.

How wrong they are. Barak's overgenerous offer to [Yasser] Arafat at Camp David II was rejected, resulting, prior to Rosh Hashanah, in an unprecedented Arab insurrection with a repeat of violence and terrorism unseen in the history of Israel. The goal in this case, as it was between 1948–1967, is the demise of Israel. But this time the aggressor is being portrayed by the media (and thus the international community) as the victim—and Israel's image and reputation is becoming tarnished beyond belief.

Barak's attempt to subdue this insurrection by giving a multitude of warnings to the Palestine Liberation Organization (PLO) to cease the violence or else Israel would strike back with great force failed because the threat was not carried out; he eventually recommended negotiations with Arafat even when there was no cease-fire, increasing the prospect of the abandonment of the Temple Mount and the demise of Israel as a sovereign and viable state.

Violence Against Israelis

Here are some statistics to remind those who have forgotten. Between May 1950 (when the armistice lines were guaranteed by the great powers—now we are currently witnessing an attempt of a repeat performance) and October 1953, 421 Israelis were killed or wounded, there were 128 acts of sabotage involving explosives, and 866 armed attacks. Or perhaps we should refer to 1955 as a typical year in which there were 257 Israeli casualties along the so-called cease-fire lines, including 75 dead, 179 wounded, and 3 taken prisoner. One can ask where did these terrorists come from, and why were the armistice agreements broken by the Arab countries—just like the PLO is repeating today? Egypt and Gaza were the source of 53 percent of the terrorist attacks, Jordan (including the West Bank) 23 percent, Syria 22 percent, and Lebanon 2 percent. All of this was before the "occupation," where there was no alien Israeli force imposing its will on the Arab population, unlike that practiced by the US on occupied Germany and Japan after World War II.

On 13 October 1953, a mother and her two children were murdered in their sleep on Moshav Yahud, just south of Petach Tikvah. Tracks led across the nearby border to the West Bank village of Rantis. In December of that year, a member of Kibbutz Ein Shemer was shot by infiltrators while walking near Karkur in central Israel. In March 1954, Arab gunmen ambushed and attacked an Israeli bus at Malei Akribim, south of Beersheva, murdering 11 including women and children. If that is not sufficient, consider June 1954: Jerusalem suddenly became a target—Jordanian machine guns, rifles, grenades, and two-inch mortars opened fire from the Old City walls. This continued for hours and was repeated several days later. Casualties—four dead, 27 wounded.

Exposing Israelis to More Danger

Of course, events like these don't tell the whole story, for there were hundreds of instances like these where the Israeli Defense Forces succeeded in foiling such attacks. And so it went on, day by day, for years. On other occasions the Fedayin crossed nearby truce lines, sup-posedly patroled by the UN and guaranteed by the Great Powers, to carry out their deadly missions. Is this not a repeat of what is now being seen?—freight trains blown up, farmers murdered in their fields, soldiers ambushed and killed, children attacked by snipers, mines laid as gangs come across to burn, kill, steal, and destroy.

How easy it was in those days. One has to reflect that the width of Israel was in some places less than 15 miles from the cease-fire line between Israel and occupied West Bank, and the whole of the central Shomron Plain was exposed to these people—as it will be again if [the land for peace] policy continues.

What did they want in those days? Before the talk of land for peace, they already occupied the West Bank under Jordanian rule and Gaza under Egyptian rule.

Those who now subscribe to land for peace . . . say there should be a return to the good old days of 1967, because there is no choice. Do they recollect that every Israeli was within firing distance of hostile Arabs either in the West Bank or Gaza, never mind the Golan Heights? There are families today in Israel who mourn members who were killed going around carrying out their peaceful occupations. The list is tragically long. It is time to remember that Israel was not then an occupying power. But this did not deter the Arabs. It is the same old story; those who carried out the mass pogroms in Hebron in 1929, who carried out a bloody swath in the 1936–1939 period, who collab-orated with Hitler, and who tried to destroy the infant state before its birth in 1948 are still active.

Jews Have Given Too Much Land

The Jewish people have been giving land for peace from the time of World War I and the Balfour Declaration. The original territory assigned by the 52 members of the League of Nations in 1920 extended to 43,075 sq. miles, extending to both banks of the Jordan. The land was subsequently partitioned illegally by the British, grant-ing Arabs the territory of Trans-Jordan (now the Hashemite Kingdom) amounting to 32,460 sq. miles, reducing the size for a Jewish home-land to 10,615 sq. miles, less than 25 percent of the available territory. Was this insufficient for the Arabs? Of course not! But the world thought it was, when they voted on 29 November 1947 in the UN for the establishment of a Jewish State and for further partitioning of the territory, reducing the Jewish area to 5,560 sq. miles, approximately 13 percent of the original land. This was accepted by the Jews but rejected by the Arabs who promised to wage a war of extermination and momentous massacre which would be spoken of like the Mongo-lian massacres and the Crusades.

Not to be forgotten is the double relinquishing to Egypt of 23,622 sq. miles of Sinai, apart from the additional 618 sq. miles west of the

Suez Canal that were conquered in the counteroffensive in 1973, in exchange for a cold peace which is day-by-day switching into open hostility. Yet today the Egyptian government is promulgating a level of anti-semitism not seen since the Nazi era, threatening war with Israel should more land not be ceded, and denying the Jewish sanctity of the Temple Mount in Jerusalem claiming it is a myth. Making border modifications with Jordan has not brought around any Jordanian concessions—King Abdullah now promulgates the demand of total Israeli withdrawal from land that the Jordanians illegally occupied from 1948 to 1967, even though his father relinquished Jordanian rights to the land. As far as Abdullah is concerned, he demands Israel return to the good old days before 1967 when Jordan failed to implement the Freedom of Access to Jews to Holy sites, just as we now see history repeating itself with the actions of the Palestinian Authority (PA) in Shechem and Aza.

Barak is prepared to assign away Jewish rights to such Holy Sites to the PA. Even the redefining of the Lebanese border in 2000 has seen Israel conceding more land than that required by not sticking to a correct definition of which international border to use.

In the meantime, the Arabs who control 5,345,000 sq. miles have yet to relinquish one single grain of Arab soil as a confidence-building measure towards peaceful coexistence with the Jewish state. The world, through the media, has been duped into supporting the rights of the Arabs and fails to acknowledge any Jewish rights. When Egypt was negotiating over the final Israeli withdrawal from land at Taba in Sinai, they were resolute not to cede one grain of what they described as holy Arab soil. . . .

Land for Peace Will Not Work

Faisal Husseini stated unequivocally that the current insurrection is a war of independence, and in a few years "Palestinians" will be a majority, and they will decide whether to grant Israelis a state. Yet Barak is oblivious to such threats and is prepared to cede land until the borders of Israel are reduced to the 1947 partition lines with our holy city ruled by non-Jews whose claims are falsely based.

So to . . . those who subscribe to the notion of Land for Peace: They should reconsider their simplistic solution, just withdraw and give away the land to the PLO. Camp David II was certainly not the last chance, as Barak would have had the world believe before its "failure." No man is indispensable, no date is sacrosanct, and there are certainly alternative choices as to which course of action to follow as well. Too many times in the past have the Jewish people followed the policy of appeasement with dire consequences. Even in England, Jews were expelled 1000 years ago because they appeased the rulers by providing funds which the latter were subsequently unable and unwilling to pay back—followed by massacres and expulsion; they probably subscribed to the Yihiyeh B'seder (it will be OK) policy. The major group of world powers have their own agendas to follow, which certainly does not include the survival of a Jewish state in Eretz Yisrael. They have been put to the test too often and have failed every time. Withdrawal must not be at the expense of a secure Israel firmly established in Eretz Yisrael.

We must stand firm, without weak hearts. And we must convince the world now. In order to achieve this, we must root out doubt and the spirit of defeatism and appeasement in our own midst.

THE UNITED STATES SHOULD IMPLEMENT A SETTLEMENT

Sherwin Wine

Rabbi Sherwin Wine is the founder of the Humanist Institute, the Society for Humanistic Judaism, and the International Association of Humanist Educators, Counselors, and Leaders. He also serves as the cochair of the International Institute for Secular Humanistic Judaism. According to Wine, too much suspicion and hatred exists between Arabs and Jews for them to successfully negotiate a peace agreement for the Middle East. Instead, he contends, the United States should step in and impose a settlement between the Israelis and the Palestinians. This way, Wine suggests, the leaders of both sides can blame the United States for any concessions they are forced to make, enabling them to save face with their constituencies. The author writes that an imposed settlement must include particular parameters, including erecting a fence between Jewish and Palestinian territories, establishing East Jerusalem as the Palestinian capital, and removing most Jewish settlements from the West Bank and the Gaza Strip.

The war between the Jews and the Arabs in former British Palestine has been going on for eighty-one years. In 1921, the first Arab explosion against the Zionist pioneers announced the beginning of the fray. Hatred and suspicion have undermined any successful resolution of the conflict.

After the Jewish War of Independence in 1948, the conflict became a war between the Jewish state and external Arab enemies. In that conflict, the Israelis were generally victorious. The Israeli triumph in 1967 crushed Gamal Abdel Nasser, the hero of Arab nationalism. But in 1987 the Palestinian Arabs chose a new kind of battle—internal rebellion. The infitada was born. And it has grown in fury ever since.

The Power of Nationalism

The foundation of the war is the power of nationalism. Jewish nationalism was born out of the defiance of the oppressed masses in czarist

Sherwin Wine, "Arabs and Jews: Is There Any Light at the End of the Tunnel for Peace in the Middle East? Or Is the Jewish-Arab War Condemned to Last Forever?" *Humanist*, vol. 62, September/October 2002, p. 15. Copyright © 2002 by American Humanist Association. Reproduced by permission.

Russia. It was fed by racial anti-Semitism. Diaspora nationalism sought to liberate the Jews of eastern Europe and give them cultural autonomy. It was destroyed by native resistance and the Holocaust.

Zionist nationalism also saw itself as a national liberation movement. It naively proposed to solve anti-Semitism by returning the Jews to their ancient homeland. Reinforced by socialist idealism and the revival of Hebrew as a popular language, it led to the establishment of a Jewish settlement in Palestine. The closing of the doors to immigration in the United States, the support of the British government, and the rise of Adolf Hitler gave this nationalism the impetus that the slaughter of six million Jews was to make irresistible. Zionism became the most powerful movement to mobilize the Jewish masses in the twentieth century.

Arab nationalism was an import from the West and was cultivated initially by Christian Arabs as a way of countering their exclusion by Muslims. Propelled by Turkish oppression and by the humiliation of European conquest, the Arab nationalist movement was led by Westernized intellectuals who embraced secular values and placed nationhood above religion. Since the Arab world never fully experienced the secular revolution which had transformed European life, the Arab nationalism of the street had difficulty distinguishing between Arab loyalty and Muslim loyalty. Religion is inevitably part of the nationalist package in the Muslim world.

Since the Arab world is vast, divided by regional differences, cultural diversity, and the internal boundaries of twenty-two states created by colonial masters, the unification of the Arab nation hasn't been easy. Nasser tried and failed. He was defeated by both the Israelis and by the hostility of his political enemies and rivals within the Arab world.

Hatred Between Jews and Arabs

The one issue that has the power to transcend the internal state boundaries of the Arab world and to mobilize the Arab masses is Zionism. Whether or not it deserves such designation, the Jewish state has become the symbol of Arab humiliation. Perceived as the last and most outrageous example of European colonialism, Israel is the object of almost universal Arab hate. The defeat of Israel has become the ultimate perceived means of restoring Arab honor. The hatred of Zionism is so intense that it is difficult for most Arabs to distinguish between their hostility to Israel and their hatred for Jews.

In fact, the suspicion and hatred between Arabs and Jews is so fierce that dialogue is condemned to failure. Most public and private encounters between conventional Arab and Jewish leaders degenerate into shouting matches. Each side insists on its rights. And, of course, both sides are "right." The Palestinian Arabs have been invaded, abused, and oppressed. The Israeli Jews are by now mainly native-born residents of the land they defend and the creators of a dynamic, modern, high-tech state; they have no place else to go.

From the Jewish point of view, the Arab hostility cannot easily be distinguished from anti-Semitism. The memories of the Holocaust hover over every response. Of course, the popular media in the Arab world reinforce this perception by aping the propaganda of European Jew hatred. From the perspective of the Arabs, Jewish voices are confused with the voices of Jewish extremists who advocate expulsion and deportation.

There is an abundance of extremists on both sides. The Arab and Palestinian nationalist and fundamentalist worlds feature many militant groups that advocate terrorism and call for the destruction of the Jewish state. The Jewish and Israeli extremists are equally militant in their refusal to recognize the right of a Palestinian state to exist (beyond suggesting that Jordan is already a Palestinian state). To the credit of the Israelis, Israel features a peace movement that has no counterpart in the Arab world.

Victims on Every Side

Both sides see themselves as victims. Jews see Israel as a small beleaguered state in a vast and petroleum-rich Arab world that does nothing to rescue its Palestinian brothers and sisters from poverty. Arabs see Israel as the agent of American imperialism, supported by the wealth and military technology of the world's only superpower—a nation that is beholden to Jewish political power.

The failure of the Oslo peace process is as much the result of intense hatred and suspicion as it is the incompatibility of vested interests. The issues of boundaries, Jerusalem, and refugees are shrouded by such levels of distrust that the normal compromises that negotiations bring can never emerge. No arrangements can provide the security that most Israelis want. And no "deal" can yield the sense of honor and vindication that most Palestinians and Arabs seek.

In searching for alternatives to endless war, certain realities need to be confronted. This war is not only bad for the Israelis and the Palestinians but also for Jews and Arabs. For the Jews, the war has already spread to Europe, where Muslim militants assault synagogues and vulnerable Jews. For the Arabs, the war prevents any real confrontation with the political, economic, and social issues that affect their world. War continues to justify government by military dictators.

This war is bad for the United States and the rest of the world. The Palestinian issue has provided the fuel whereby Muslim militants have won the allegiance of millions of Arabs and Muslims in their desire to wage war against the United States and Western culture. A war between the West and Islam is a world war. It is different from a war against Muslim fundamentalist terrorism; such a conflict would enjoy the support of most Muslim governments. The success of the United States' response to the attacks of September 11, 2001, lies in the ability to make such a distinction.

Jews and Arabs, Israelis and Palestinians by themselves cannot achieve peace—or even an effective truce—by relying on negotiations alone; the cycle of vengeance has its own logic. Every terrorist action incites retaliation; every retaliation incites counter-retaliation. No antagonist can allow itself to be seen as weak. Revenge is a necessary tactic in maintaining credibility. The cycle cannot stop itself without outside intervention.

The proposed Palestinian state is no more than 3,000 square miles in size—hardly a formula for viability. It is presently a series of urban "doughnut holes" within Israeli-occupied territory. The presence of the Israeli army is justified not only by the argument for security but also by the necessity to defend small Jewish settlements which have been established in the West Bank and Gaza by religious Jewish settlers laying claim to the land. These settlements prevent peace, add nothing to the security of Israel, and provide more provocation to Arabs to kill more Jews.

Jerusalem is already divided. Jewish Jerusalem (about two-thirds of the expanded city) has no Arabs, while Arab Jerusalem (the eastern sector) has no Jews. While some Arabs work in Jewish Jerusalem, almost no Jews even penetrate Arab Jerusalem unless they are on military duty. A unified city is more desirable than a divided city, but the division already exists.

A binational Israeli-Palestinian state—a dream of many peaceniks—is not politically viable even though it would be economically desirable. Jewish and Arab nationalism are realities; they cannot be wished away. Mutual hatred and suspicion are realities; they cannot be dismissed. Arguing against nationalism may work a hundred years from now but it doesn't fly today. A Jewish state—in which Jewish national culture is the dominant culture and most people speak Hebrew—is no more racist than would be an Arab state whose dominant culture and language reflected its people. Three million Palestinian refugees cannot return to the Jewish state without destroying the Jewish national character of the Jewish state.

The United States Must Intervene

Because outside intervention is required, the only superpower capable of orchestrating it successfully is the United States. Since September 11, George W. Bush has mobilized an effective coalition of world powers, including Europe, Russia, China, and India—as well as many allies in the Muslim world. The war between the Israelis and the Palestinians has begun to undermine the coalition, especially with Bush's perceived support of the Ariel Sharon government in Israel. Joint intervention with the approval of the United Nations and with the support of moderate Muslim powers could restore the coalition. This intervention is no different from the intervention that the United

States initiated in Bosnia and Kosovo.

What would be the elements of such an intervention? The United States controls the process. The Israelis don't trust the United Nations and won't cooperate with an effort managed by the hostile nations of the developing world.

The United States acts as a neutral "parent." It doesn't always praise one side and condemn the other; it creates a setting for negotiations, with the presence of major members of the coalition. The format of such negotiations is only a pretense. In the "back room" the United States dictates the settlement and everybody knows that the United States has imposed the settlement. Both antagonists protest, but they yield because they have no choice. The imposition gives the leaders of both sides an excuse, a way to save face, and a scapegoat. They can justify their "surrender" to their constituencies by pleading helplessness. They may even shake hands reluctantly. Whether [Yasser] Arafat will still be representing the Palestinians is the question.

Requirements for an Effective Settlement

All that can realistically be achieved at this time is an effective truce. Peace will have to await a reduction in the fury of hatred and suspicion. For now, an imposed settlement should include the following:

- the removal of all Jewish settlements from the West Bank and Gaza, except those settlements which function as contiguous communities for Tel Aviv and Jerusalem
- the digging of a ditch and construction of a fence between the Jews and Arabs along the adjusted 1967 boundaries
- the policing of this fence by the United States and its European allies
- the granting of Arab East Jerusalem to the Palestinians as their national capital
- the demilitarization of the new Palestinian state, with periodic inspections by the United States and its coalition partners
- compensation for Palestinian refugees who cannot return.

Such compensation may cost over $30 billion and would be covered by the United States, Japan, and European allies. If the compensation helps to bring about an effective truce, it would be worth the investment. Rescuing the global economy for peace justifies the expense.

Israel needs to be compensated for its "willingness" to shrink and to confront the wrath of its right-wing extremists. Since it won't in the foreseeable future be accepted by the Arab and Muslim worlds, it needs to be regarded as the European power it is. Israel's high-tech economy needs the European market, just as its European culture needs a European support system. The price that Europe pays for this necessary peace is that it accepts Israel as a member of the European Union. Such acceptance is no different than acceptance of Cyprus or Turkey, and Israelis will be better off trading in euros than shekels.

After this settlement is imposed, terrorist violence will likely continue. The war against Muslim fundamentalist terrorists will also continue. For the extremists in the Arab and Muslim world—and even in the Jewish world—hatred is a way of life. For moderates, an effective truce will enable them to join the forces of peace.

The ball is in Bush's court if he would only lead the way. The leaders of the Defense Department and the religious right will likely oppose this kind of proposal, but only such action can provide any light at the end of the tunnel that is the Middle East.

WHAT WE CAN DO

Henry A. Kissinger

In the following selection, former U.S. secretary of state Henry A. Kissinger argues that America should take on the role of a mediator in the Arab-Israeli conflict. While he acknowledges that U.S. diplomacy has played a large part in the peace process so far, Kissinger asserts that the breakdown of the Camp David talks in 2000 has created an environment in which American attempts to negotiate a final settlement are doomed to fail. Instead, he proposes that for the immediate future, the United States should concentrate on managing the current crisis by helping Israel and Palestine to agree on attainable goals and to establish a cease-fire. A limited settlement in which neither side achieves all of its aims, Kissinger writes, will create a state of compromise that will increase the likelihood that later negotiations will be more successful. Kissinger is currently the head of Kissinger Associates, a private consulting firm.

The reappearance of active American diplomacy in the Middle East has been greeted with a mixture of hope and trepidation. Hope, because the rage of both parties is giving way to exhaustion. Trepidation, because both sides know their objectives to be essentially incompatible. The secret dream of Israelis is legitimization of the status quo. For Palestinians, the goal is the imposition of terms reducing Israel to its 1967 borders, which could facilitate the destruction of the Jewish state.

Many who generally criticize America's foreign policy (and count among our sins obliviousness to their advice) are joining the widespread call for Washington to play a dominant role. These pleas have been given fresh impetus by the initiative of Crown Prince Abdullah of Saudi Arabia, which proposes normalization of relations between the Arab world and Israel if Israel returns to the 1967 frontiers. Thus Vice President Dick Cheney's journey to the Middle East, intended to elicit Arab support for a possible showdown with Iraq, was reshaped by his Arab hosts into an occasion for a new initiative to end the Arab-Israeli conflict. This deflection of attention from terrorism to the Palestinian issue is in itself a considerable achievement for Saudi diplomacy. At the same time, the near unanimity in Europe and the Arab world urging American intervention stems from the hope that, in the end, we will impose on Israel a settlement essentially identical to the Abdullah plan.

In the past 30 years, American diplomacy has been the catalyst for practically all the progress the peace process made. But given the explosive politics of the region, it is all too easy to overestimate what is possible. In 2000, the impetuous attempt to settle all issues in one negotiation of limited duration at Camp David contributed to the outbreak of the current warfare.

In present conditions, a comparison of both sides' positions demonstrates that another attempt at a negotiated final solution would not fare better. The only formal plan by an Israeli government was put forward by Prime Minister Ehud Barak at Camp David. In it, he offered more than 90 percent of the disputed territories (the formula was complex) but retained about 70 percent of the settlements. In exchange, the Palestinians were asked to renounce any future claims, including the right to return into Israel proper (though they would be free to return to a Palestinian state). Prime Minister Ariel Sharon has disavowed this proposal. Yasir Arafat preferred the intifada to the implications of finality.

The most forthcoming Arab proposal has come from Crown Prince Abdullah. According to its imprecise outline, Israel would return to the dividing lines of 1967 in exchange for the normalization of relations with the Arab states. Literally, this would imply Israeli abandonment of all settlements and Arab control of the Old City of Jerusalem, including the holy places. The Abdullah plan does not define what is meant by normalization, and is silent about such issues as the right of refugees to return (though it would surely be insisted on in an actual negotiation).

Welcome as this engagement in the peace process is—the first by an Arab state not having a direct national conflict with Israel—its specific terms represent a restatement of a position that has produced the existing deadlock. The pre-1967 "border" in Palestine—unlike the Egyptian, Syrian or Jordanian frontiers with Israel—was never an international frontier but a ceasefire line established at the end of the 1948 war. It was never recognized by any Arab state until after the 1967 war and has been grudgingly accepted recently by states that do not yet recognize the legitimacy of Israel. I have never encountered an Israeli prime minister or chief of staff who considered the '67 borders defensible, and especially if coupled with an abandonment of a security position along the Jordan River. This is because the '67 borders leave a corridor as narrow as eight miles between Haifa and Tel Aviv and put the border of Israel at the edge of its international airport. Moreover, Israel would have to give up settlements containing approximately 200,000 inhabitants (about 4 percent of its Jewish population).

In return, Israel would achieve diplomatic relations with its neighbors. But in almost all other negotiations, mutual recognition of the parties is taken for granted, not treated as a concession. In fact, nonrecognition implies the legal nonexistence of the other state, which, in the context of the Middle East, is tantamount to an option to destroy it. Once granted, recognition can always be withdrawn; breaking diplomatic relations is a recognized diplomatic tool. Nor does formal normalization involve much else: Israel's peace agreement with Egypt of 23 years ago has brought little in the way of enhanced economic or cultural relations other than an exchange of ambassadors who are rarely brought into play.

While the terms of the crown prince's proposal represent no breakthrough, Saudi engagement could be important if it is used to produce a ceasefire and to start negotiations without preconditions from either side. But if its ultimate purpose is to induce the United States to impose its specific provisions, it would undermine the security of Israel and ultimately the stability of the region.

The precariousness of Israel's position is paradoxical. Israel has never been more powerful, and at the same time never more vulnerable. Israel is militarily stronger than any conceivable Arab adversary; it is clearly able to inflict heavy losses on Palestinian terrorist groups. But it has evolved into a middle-class advanced society and, as such, the strain of guerrilla warfare is psychologically draining. The intifada has generated an ambivalent rigidity in Israeli society. Prior to the Oslo agreement, the Israeli peace movement viewed reconciliation with the Arab world primarily in terms of psychological reassurance; land would be traded for peace even though the Arab quid pro quo would be revocable. But since the intifada, the vast majority of Israelis no longer believe in reconciliation; they want victory and the crushing of their Arab adversaries.

At the same time, there is growing despair over the seeming futility of the enterprise. With the proportion of Israeli casualties to that of the guerrillas going up, and the fact that Israel's retaliation beyond a certain point will not be tolerated by the United States, a sense of resignation is spreading. The desire to turn on the tormentors is beginning to be offset by signs of a hunger for peace at any price.

Israel finds itself facing the classic dynamic of guerrilla warfare as it has played out for two generations now. The guerrillas not only do not recoil from terrorism but practice an egregious form of it because a violent, emotional (and to bystanders), excessive retaliation serves their purpose: to trigger intervention by the international community, especially the United States. In the process, sanctuaries are established—however dubious their basis in international law—that, to all practical purposes, eliminate the capacity of the defending forces to get to the root of the guerrilla challenge. That process gradually erodes Israel's margin of survival even while the world's media and diplomats bewail its excesses. Torn between a recognition of strategic necessities and the pull of emotional imperatives, Israel runs the risk of sliding into paralysis.

Yet the imposition of the indefensible '67 frontiers is not the solution. For after the experiences of Oslo, Israelis know (as should the rest of the world) that the real division among Palestinians is not between those who want peace in the Western sense—as a point after which the world lives free of tensions with a consciousness of reconciliation. In reality, the number of Palestinian leaders holding this view is minuscule. The fundamental schism is between those who want to bring about the destruction of Israel by continuing the present struggle, and those who believe that an agreement now would be a better strategy to rally forces for the ultimate showdown later on.

Even if those Palestinians who sign a "final" agreement have no afterthoughts, no one can guarantee that they will not be replaced by radical successors. A peace agreement will not quell but may stimulate the intransigence of Hamas and other radical groups or states. If, as is asserted, Arafat cannot be asked to accept a permanent ceasefire as an entrance price into negotiations because his radical opponents would have a veto, why would not the same condition apply after a peace settlement? Thus the differences between a permanent and an interim settlement are more a matter of adjectives than substance.

NATO, American or other third-party guarantees are of marginal utility in overcoming this problem. Nobody can seriously believe that the European countries would go to war for Israel, especially against challenges that are likely to be ambiguous. The only possible solution would be an American guarantee against invasion from neighboring states. Aside from raising profound domestic questions in the United States, this would bring with it an American veto of Israeli retaliation against less than all-out attack and be almost impossible to apply against the resumption of guerrilla warfare.

Therefore, the beginning of wisdom is to recognize the impossibility of a final settlement under current conditions. Some crises can only be managed, not solved. The constant invocation of unattainable goals will foster a general climate of irresponsibility. Yet a less ambitious mediation may have some prospects, if for no other reason than that the status quo is becoming increasingly intolerable for Palestinians as well. They have fought ferociously on behalf of the classic paradigm of asymmetrical warfare: the guerrilla wins if he does not lose. Still, a point may be approaching where the costs of the war exhaust, or perhaps even destroy, the civil society the guerrillas are seeking to establish. For the other Arab states, their impotence on the Palestine issue threatens in time to radicalize their domestic politics. They have a stake in a truce even if they are not able for domestic reasons to support an overall settlement on meaningful terms.

But before the United States launches itself into a major diplomatic effort, it must be clear about what is at stake. Will the mediation be interpreted in the region as being produced by terrorism, or as an attempt to shape an outcome based on familiar American principles? Will the perceived lesson be that September 11 in the end obliged America to adopt positions it had rejected previously? Or will terrorism be viewed as obstructing rather than inspiring a positive American role? If negotiations start, will the military prowess displayed by the Palestinians in the intifada provide an excuse for Arafat to play the constructive role Anwar Sadat did after the temporary Arab successes of the 1973 war? Or will he view America in retreat and Israel on the verge of an abyss—toward which he will push it step by step with the help of outside mediation? The answers to these questions will determine the prospects for a peaceful evolution of the region, and also to a large extent the prospects for America's war against terrorism.

The Palestinians will not accept a ceasefire because they believe they have momentum; the Israelis will not yield because they fear for their existence. America can bridge this gap only by making clear to both sides that the only feasible goal is a limited settlement in which each will achieve less than its maximum aim but more than it can accomplish by a continuation of the conflict. It must urge Israel toward a peace program; it must impress upon its Arab interlocutors the limits of achievable concessions.

The strength of the Bush administration has been to cut through slogans to underlying realities. Under present circumstances, this means insisting that a ceasefire must accompany negotiations and that negotiations must aim for less than a final settlement. The goal of such an agreement would be to secure borders for a Palestinian state with contiguous territory. As part of the necessary withdrawals Israel should be prepared to abandon outlying settlements. Issues other than the border between the two states would be left for later negotiations. There should be an interval of sufficient length for normal life to resume on both sides, encouraged by outside economic assistance. The United States should play a major role in facilitating such an outcome, provided the parties agree to the principles embodied in it. In its absence the United States has no option except to stand aside. If the United States appears to be gradually veering toward imposing the '67 borders, it risks continuation of the conflict.

To contribute to genuine progress, America must back a program that combines respect for Arab dignity with Israel's necessities for survival. There is no middle way.

GLOSSARY

aliyah: Immigration by Jews to Israel.

Allah: God.

Fatah: A network of Palestinian nationalist groups, each with its own leader.

fatwa: An interpretation of Islamic religious law issued by an authoritative scholar or leader.

Gaza Strip: Along with the **West Bank**, one of the occupied territories seized by Israel in the Six-Day War in 1967.

hadith: Traditional accounts of sayings or actions by the Islamic prophet Muhammad and his companions, which are referred to for authoritative precedent in interpreting the **Koran**.

Hamas: Literally, an acronym standing for the Arabic words for "Islamic Resistance Movement"; a militant guerrilla group in **Gaza** and the **West Bank** that refuses to recognize or negotiate with Israel.

Hezbollah: (sometimes Hizballah) Literally, "Party of **Allah**"; an Islamic political party in Lebanon that has been accused of terrorism.

intifada: An uprising; refers most often to the uprising of Palestinians in the **West Bank** and **Gaza Strip** that began in December 1987.

Irgun: An underground, militant **Zionist** group that was active mainly during the time of British control of Palestine.

Islam: Submission to God and to God's message revealed to Muhammad; the religion of **Muslims**.

Islamic Jihad: A militant group that believes the liberation of Palestine will lead to the unification of the Arab and **Muslim** worlds.

Israeli Defense Force: The Israeli military.

Jewish Defense League: An organization that urges Jews to immigrate to Israel and advocates the removal of all Arabs from the **West Bank**.

Jewish National Fund: A fund established in 1901 for the purpose of purchasing land in Palestine.

jihad: Literally, a struggle; can refer to any struggle, from a personal striving to fulfill religious responsibilities to a holy war undertaken for the defense of **Islam**.

kibbutz: A communally operated Jewish settlement, typically agricultural.

Knesset: The Israeli Parliament.

Koran: (often Quran) Literally, "the recitation"; the Holy Book of the Islamic faith, containing the revelations and prophecies of Muhammad.

Labor: An Israeli political party, generally characterized as liberal.

Likud: An Israeli political party, generally characterized as conservative.

Meretz: The Israeli Social Democratic and Peace-Seeking Party; a political party dedicated to protecting human rights and creating peace for Israel, with Arabs and Jews working together.

Mizrahi: (plural: Mizrahim) A Jew of African or Asian origin.

Muslim: (sometimes Moslem) A person who follows the Islamic faith, encompassing the teachings of Muhammad.

Palestine Liberation Organization (PLO): An organization created in 1964 by Arab states to unite and control various Palestinian guerrilla groups.

Palestinian Authority (PA): (sometimes Palestinian National Authority) The Palestinian governmental body established in 1994 to administer portions of the **West Bank** and **Gaza Strip**.

Palestinian National Council (PNC): The legislative arm of the **Palestine Liberation Organization**.

Resolution 194: A resolution passed by the United Nations in 1948, stating that Palestinian refugees have an "inalienable right" to return to their homes in Israel.

Resolution 242: A resolution passed by the United Nations in 1967 after the Six-Day War, urging Israel to withdraw from recently occupied territories and calling for recognition of the sovereignty and independence of all nations in the region.

Resolution 338: A resolution passed by the United Nations in 1973, calling for direct negotiations between Israel and the Arab states to implement Resolution 242.

seder: A ceremonial dinner held by Jews on the first night of Passover.

shahid: A martyr.

shivah: (often shiva) The traditional Jewish week of mourning.

Sukkot: A Jewish harvest festival that commemorates the period after the exodus from Egypt, during which Jews wandered in the wilderness and lived in temporary shelters.

surah: A chapter of the **Koran**.

Talmud: A collection of Jewish law consisting of the Mishnah and the Gemara, produced between A.D. 400–500.

Tanzim: Literally, "organization"; a militia operating under the control of the **Fatah**.

Torah: The five books of Moses (roughly corresponding to the first five books of the Christian Old Testament); also, the entire body of Jewish wisdom and law as contained in Jewish scripture and other sacred or traditional literature.

West Bank: Along with the **Gaza Strip**, one of the occupied territories seized by Israel in the Six-Day War in 1967.

Zionism: The historical worldwide movement that promoted the establishment of a permanent national homeland for Jews in Palestine.

CHRONOLOGY

1881
Russian pogroms force thousands of Jews to move west. Leo Pinsker founds the Hibbat Zion movement, which urges persecuted Jews to settle Palestine as a national homeland.

1882
A student society establishes Rishon le Zion, the first Zionist settlement in Palestine. Several other colonies are founded soon after.

1897
Theodor Herzl convenes the First Zionist Congress, which designates Palestine as an appropriate Jewish homeland. Less than 10 percent of Palestine's population is Jewish.

1915
Sir Henry McMahon enlists the support of the Arabs in Britain's World War I effort against Turkey by promising British approval of a unified Arab nation. Arab nationalists later argue this promise includes Palestine; the British maintain Palestine must be an exception to Arab rule.

November 2, 1917
In a statement that becomes known as the Balfour Declaration, British foreign secretary A.J. Balfour announces Britain's support for a national homeland for the Jewish people in Palestine.

December 9, 1917
Allied forces advance into Jerusalem during World War I and force the city's surrender, ending four hundred years of Turkish rule.

1920–1948
Britain rules Palestine under an agreement with the League of Nations. The British mandate approves limited immigration for Jews.

1929–1939
Arabs rebel against British rule; Arabs and Jews fight each other for the right to live in Palestine.

1930
The British government, reacting to Arab riots against Jewish immigration, publishes the Passfield White Paper, which advocates restriction of Jewish immigration and land sales in Palestine.

1937
A British Royal Commission, headed by Lord Peel, reports that Arab and Jewish national aspirations are irreconcilable and recommends the partition of Palestine.

1939
The British tighten limits of Jewish immigration into Palestine.

1939–1945
During World War II, six million Jews are killed by Nazi Germany. The Jewish population in Palestine swells to 608,000 by 1946.

1945–1948
Zionist organizations wage a campaign of violence to end immigration restrictions in Palestine; thousands of Jews enter Palestine illegally.

November 29, 1947
The United Nations passes Resolution 181, which mandates the partition of Palestine into Jewish and Arab states, with Jerusalem being an international city. Arabs reject the plan.

May 14, 1948
David Ben-Gurion, Israel's first prime minister, proclaims the nation of Israel, which is immediately attacked by five Arab countries. Israel defeats the coalition and takes over large tracts of the proposed Palestinisn state. Only the West Bank (under Jordanian administration) and the Gaza Strip (Egypt) remain in Arab hands. More than five hundred thousand Palestinians flee Israel.

December 11, 1948
The United Nations adopts Resolution 194, which states that Palestinian refugees have "an inalienable right" to return to their homes in Israel.

January 1950
The new Law of Return grants every Jew the right to immigrate to Israel. Israel declares Jerusalem its capital despite protest from Arab states and the United Nations.

July 1956
The United States and Britain refuse to support a loan to Egypt to build the Aswan High Dam; in retaliation, Egyptian president Gamal Abdel Nasser seizes control of the Suez Canal from its British and French owners. After Britain freezes Egyptian assets held in England, Egypt closes the canal.

October 29, 1956
The Israelis, with military aid from Britain and France, invade Egypt. They take the Gaza Strip and the Sinai Peninsula, which they later return in a peace settlement.

June 1964
Arab leaders convene in Jerusalem and create the Palestine Liberation Organization (PLO) nationalist movement. The Palestine National Charter calls for the PLO to engage in armed struggle to "liquidate the Zionist presence in Palestine." Yasser Arafat's Fatah group carries out its first raid on Israel the following year.

May 1967
Nasser orders UN emergency forces to withdraw from the Sinai, declares a state of emergency in the Gaza Strip, and closes the Strait of Tiran to shipping to and from Israel. Israel and the United States warn Egypt to remove the blockade.

June 5–10, 1967
Six-Day War. Israel attacks Egypt, Syria, and Jordan in what it calls a preemp-

tive strike, capturing the Sinai Peninsula and Gaza Strip from Egypt, the Golan Heights from Syria, and the West Bank and East Jerusalem from Jordan. One million Arabs living in the captured territories come under Israeli rule.

November 22, 1967
The UN Security Council adopts Resolution 242, calling for Israeli withdrawal from territory taken in the Six-Day War, recognition of all states in the region, and a just settlement of the Palestinian refugee problem.

1969
The Fatah faction takes control of the PLO; Arafat becomes PLO chairman.

October 6, 1973
Yom Kippur War. Egypt and Syria launch a two-front surprise attack on Israeli forces in the Sinai Peninsula and the Golan Heights on the holiest day of the Jewish calendar.

October 18, 1973
First day of a five-month Arab oil embargo cutting off or sharply curtailing oil exports to countries that support Israel.

October 22, 1973
The UN Security Council adopts Resolution 338, which calls for an immediate cease-fire, the beginning of peace negotiations, and the implementation of Resolution 242.

November 11, 1973
Egypt and Israel agree to a cease-fire.

October 1974
The United Nations grants the PLO observer status and allows it to participate in debates on the status of Palestinian refugees.

November 1975
The UN General Assembly adopts a resolution equating Zionism with racism.

November 1977
Egyptian president Anwar Sadat makes the first visit of an Arab leader to Israel to promote renewed peace talks. In exchange for peace, Israel offers to return Sinai to Egypt and allow limited Palestinian self-rule in the Israeli-occupied areas of the West Bank and Gaza Strip.

September 5–17, 1978
The Camp David summit meeting between U.S. president Jimmy Carter, Israeli prime minister Menachem Begin, and Sadat leads to an Egyptian-Israeli peace agreement and accords on the Palestinian question. Under the agreement, Israel returns all of Sinai to Egypt by 1982.

1981
Jewish settlements and housing construction begin in the West Bank.

December 14, 1981
Israel annexes the Golan Heights in Syria. The UN Security Council declares the annexation "null and void." Israel refuses to withdraw.

June–September 1982
Israel invades Lebanon; it occupies Beirut and demands that the PLO leave the city. U.S. Marines help oversee the PLO evacuation. The PLO establishes headquarters in Tunisia.

May 17, 1983
Lebanon and Israel sign an agreement to withdraw Israeli forces from Lebanon. Israel refuses to withdraw completely until Syria also withdraws.

September 1984
Shimon Peres becomes prime minister of Israel.

January 1985
Israel begins withdrawal from Lebanon and declares a nine-mile-wide security zone north of the Israeli-Lebanese border. Syria remains in control of most of Lebanon.

September 1986
Yitzhak Shamir of the conservative Likud Party replaces Peres as prime minister of Israel.

December 1987
Four Palestinians are killed when an Israeli army truck rams their car after they attempt to run a military roadblock in Gaza. During their funeral, Israeli troops clash with mourners. The event marks the beginning of the widespread Palestinian uprising that comes to be called the intifada. Hundreds of demonstrators are killed over the next five years in clashes between Israelis and Palestinians.

August 1988
King Hussein of Jordan announces the severing of legal and administrative ties to the West Bank. Jordan ceases to pay the salaries of the twenty-four thousand doctors, teachers, religious officials, and municipal employees it has maintained there. Responsibility for the West Bank's economic and municipal functions shifts to the PLO.

November 1988
The Palestine National Council (PNC) declares an independent Palestinian state.

December 13–14, 1988
The PNC accepts the original UN partition plan (Resolution 181) and UN Resolutions 242 and 338. It also accepts Israel's right to exist and renounces terrorism. The United States immediately opens formal dialogue with the PLO.

October 31–November 1, 1991
An international Middle East peace conference is convened in Madrid, Spain. The event marks the first peace negotiations ever between Israel and the Palestinians.

December 16, 1991
The UN General Assembly revokes the 1975 resolution equating Zionism with racism.

June 1992

Israel's Labor Party gains control of the government in parliamentary elections.

July 1992

Yitzhak Rabin becomes Israel's prime minister and pledges to limit construction of new Jewish settlements in the occupied territories.

December 1992

Three Israeli soldiers are killed in a drive-by shooting in the worst single attack on soldiers since the beginning of the intifada. Hamas activists kidnap and kill an Israeli border policeman. Israel arrests more than four hundred suspected Islamic militants and deports them to southern Lebanon.

January 19, 1993

Israel's parliament lifts a 1986 ban on contacts with the PLO.

February 1993

Israeli and Palestinian officials begin secret talks in Oslo, Norway.

July 25, 1993

Retaliating for the killing of seven Israeli soldiers and rocket attacks on Israeli settlements by Hezbollah, Israel launches its fiercest offense on southern Lebanon since the establishment of the border security zone. The assault kills more than one hundred Lebanese and drives more than three hundred thousand refugees northward.

August 1993

Israelis and Palestinians meeting in Oslo reach a tentative agreement for Palestinian self-rule in the occupied territories.

September 13, 1993

Arafat and Rabin sign a breakthrough Declaration of Principles, the first agreement between Israel and the PLO, which calls for Palestinian self-government initially in the Gaza Strip and the West Bank town of Jericho. The agreement sets deadlines for the resolution of other Israeli-Palestinian disputes.

October 13, 1993

Israel and the PLO open negotiations in Egypt for Palestinian self-rule.

1994

The Palestinian Authority (PA) is formed to govern the semiautonomous Palestinian state. Violence breaks out as Jewish settlers resist efforts to turn land over to the PA.

September 1995

The Israeli-Palestinian Oslo II interim agreements are signed. Oslo II divides the West Bank into three areas: one section that is to be governed by the PA, another section that is granted limited Palestinian self-rule, and a third area to remain under Israeli rule.

November 4, 1995

Rabin is assassinated by an ultra-right Israeli extremist. Peres takes over as Israel's prime minister.

May 1996
Benjamin Netanyahu is elected prime minister of Israel.

September 1996
Violence breaks out in Jerusalem after Israeli authorities open a tunnel near a Muslim holy site. More than seventy people die as a result of clashes involving protesters, Palestinian police, and Israeli soldiers.

January 1997
Israeli and Palestinian officials sign the Hebron agreement, in which Israel agrees to withdraw its forces from most of the West Bank city of Hebron and to resume Israeli military redeployment throughout the West Bank.

February 1997
Netanyahu announces the beginning of massive construction of Israeli settlements in the West Bank. Violent clashes occur between Palestinian protesters and Israeli troops, stalling peace negotiations.

October 1998
U.S., Israeli, and Arab leaders sign the Wye Memorandum, in which Israel grants Palestinians more control over the West Bank in exchange for guarantees of security and antiterrorism measures from Palestinian authorities.

December 1998
The PNC revokes clauses in its founding charter that call for Israel's destruction.

May 1999
Ehud Barak is elected prime minister of Israel.

August 2000
Arafat and Barak meet with U.S. president Bill Clinton at Camp David, Maryland, to attempt to negotiate a new peace settlement. The talks fail when Arafat refuses to accept the proposed agreement.

September 28, 2000
Israeli Parliament member Ariel Sharon visits the al-Aqsa Mosque with an armed guard. Offended Palestinians respond with violence, sparking a new intifada.

October 2000
The al-Aqsa Martyrs Brigade, a militant faction of Hamas, arises in response to the new intifada.

October 17, 2000
Meetings between Israel and the PLO in Sharm el-Sheikh, Egypt, mediated by U.S. representative George Mitchell, result in a statement known as the Mitchell Report. The report calls for a cease-fire, as well as international monitoring of the growth of Israeli settlements and Israeli enclosures of Palestinians.

January 21–27, 2001
Peace negotiations between Israelis and Palestinians take place at the resort

town of Taba, Egypt. On the eve of Israeli elections, Barak calls off the talks without any official agreements having been reached.

February 2001
Sharon is elected prime minister of Israel.

April 30, 2001
The full Mitchell Report is officially released. The document, which provides a framework for structuring potential peace talks, becomes the basis for repeated international calls for a resumption of peace negotiations between Israel and the Palestinians.

March 9, 2002
Eleven Israelis are killed at the Moment Café in Jerusalem by a suicide bomber.

March 27, 2002
Twenty-eight Jews are killed at a Passover seder in Netanya by a suicide bomber.

March 29–May 2, 2002
In an effort to restore calm and prevent further violence, Sharon orders tanks into the West Bank. Israeli forces barricade Arafat in his government compound in Ramallah. Tanks level much of the compound, but Israeli troops stop short of taking Arafat captive. The siege ends in May, and tanks withdraw from the West Bank.

April 2, 2002
Seeking to escape Israeli military incursions into the West Bank, more than two hundred Palestinian militants and bystanders take refuge in the Church of the Nativity in Bethlehem. After five weeks of negotiations, the captives are allowed to leave the church; thirteen of the gunmen are sent into exile, and twenty-six are handed over to Palestinian authorities.

March 10, 2003
In response to demands that Arafat share power in the PA, the Palestinian Legislative Council approves the creation of the position of prime minister. Arafat designates a founding member of the Fatah political party, Mahmoud Abbas (also known as Abu Mazen), as the prime minister-elect.

April 29, 2003
Abbas is officially confirmed as the Palestinian prime minister.

May 2003
New peace talks begin between Israel and the Palestinians; Sharon and Abbas agree to adhere to "the road map to peace" first proposed in the Mitchell Report.

ORGANIZATIONS TO CONTACT

The editors have compiled the following list of organizations concerned with the issues presented in this book. The descriptions are derived from materials provided by the organizations. All have publications or information available for interested readers. The list was compiled on the date of publication of the present volume; the information provided here may change. Be aware that many organizations take several weeks or longer to respond to inquiries, so allow as much time as possible.

America-Mideast Educational and Training Services (AMIDEAST)
1730 M St. NW, Suite 1100, Washington, DC 20036-4505
(202) 776-9600 • fax: (202) 776-7000
e-mail: inquiries@amideast.org • website: www.amideast.org

AMIDEAST promotes understanding and cooperation between Americans and the peoples of the Middle East and North Africa through education and development programs. It publishes the newsletter *AMIDEAST Today* and offers a number of books for all age groups, including *A History of the Modern Middle East*.

American-Israeli Cooperative Enterprise (AICE)
2810 Blaine Dr., Chevy Chase, MD 20815
(301) 565-3918 • fax: (301) 587-9056
e-mail: mgbard@aol.com • website: www.us-israel.org

AICE seeks to strengthen the U.S.-Israel relationship by emphasizing values the two nations have in common and developing cooperative social and educational programs that address shared domestic problems. It also works to enhance Israel's image by publicizing novel Israeli solutions to these problems. AICE publishes the book *Partners for Change: How U.S.-Israel Cooperation Can Benefit America*, and its website includes the Jewish Virtual Library, a comprehensive online encyclopedia of Jewish history.

American Jewish Committee (AJC)
PO Box 705, New York, NY 10150
(212) 751-4000 • fax: (212) 838-2120
e-mail: PR@ajc.org • website: www.ajc.org

AJC works to strengthen U.S.-Israel relations, build international support for Israel, and support the Israeli-Arab peace process. The committee's numerous publications include the *AJC Journal*, the report "Muslim Anti-Semitism: A Clear and Present Danger," and the papers "Iran and the Palestinian War Against Israel" and "The Arab Campaign to Destroy Israel."

Americans for Middle East Understanding (AMEU)
475 Riverside Dr., Room 245, New York, NY 10115-0245
(212) 870-2053 • fax: (212) 870-2050
e-mail: info@ameu.org • website: www.ameu.org

AMEU's purpose is to foster a better understanding in America of the history, goals, and values of Middle Eastern cultures and peoples, the rights of Palestinians, and the forces shaping U.S. policy in the Middle East. AMEU publishes *The Link*, a bimonthly newsletter, as well as books and pamphlets on the Middle East.

Arab World and Islamic Resources and School Services (AWAIR)
2137 Rose St., Berkeley, CA 94709
(510) 704-0517
e-mail: awair@igc.org • website: www.awaironline.org

AWAIR provides materials and services for educators teaching about the Arab world and Islam at the precollege level. It publishes many books and videos, including *The Arab World Studies Notebook, Middle Eastern Muslim Women Speak*, and *Palestine's Children*.

Center for Middle Eastern Studies
University of Texas, Austin, TX 78712
(512) 471-3881 • fax: (512) 471-7834
e-mail: cmes@menic.utexas.edu
website: http://menic.utexas.edu/menic/cmes

The center was established by the U.S. Department of Education to promote a better understanding of the Middle East. It provides research and instructional materials and publishes three series of books on the Middle East: the Modern Middle East series, the Middle East Monograph series, and the Modern Middle East Literatures in Translation series.

Committee for Accuracy in Middle East Reporting in America (CAMERA)
PO Box 428, Boston, MA 02258
(617) 789-3672 • fax: (617) 787-7853
e-mail: members@camera.org • website: www.camera.org

CAMERA is a nonprofit media-watch organization dedicated to promoting balanced and accurate coverage of Israel and the Middle East. Through direct responses to student inquiries and its publication *CAMERA on Campus*, it seeks to educate students about Israel, key Middle East issues, and how to respond effectively to anti-Jewish and anti-Israel incidents.

Foundation for Middle East Peace
1763 N St. NW, Washington, DC 20036
(202) 835-3650 • fax: (202) 835-3651
e-mail: info@fmep.org • website: www.fmep.org

The foundation assists the peaceful resolution of the Israeli-Palestinian conflict by making financial grants available within the Arab and Jewish communities. It publishes the bimonthly *Report on Israeli Settlements in the Occupied Territories* and additional books and papers.

Institute for Palestine Studies (IPS)
3501 M St. NW, Washington, DC 20007
(800) 874-3614 • (202) 342-3990 • fax: (202) 342-3927
e-mail: ips@ipsjps.org • website: www.ipsjps.org

IPS is a pro-Arab institute unaffiliated with any political organization or government. Established in 1963 in Beirut, the institute promotes research, analysis, and documentation of the Arab-Israeli conflict and its resolution. IPS publishes quarterlies in three languages and maintains offices all over the world. In addition to editing the *Journal of Palestine Studies*, the institute's U.S. branch publishes books and documents on the Arab-Israeli conflict and Palestinian affairs.

Middle East Institute
1761 N St. NW, Washington, DC 20036-2882
(202) 785-1141 • fax: (202) 331-8861
e-mail: mideasti@mideasti.org • website: www.themiddleeastinstitute.org

The institute's charter mission is to promote better understanding of Middle Eastern cultures, languages, religions, and politics. It publishes numerous books, papers, audiotapes, and videos as well as the quarterly *Middle East Journal*. It also maintains an Educational Outreach Department to give teachers and students of all grade levels advice on resources.

Middle East Policy Council (MEPC)
1730 M St. NW, Suite 512, Washington, DC 20036-4505
(202) 296-6767 • fax: (202) 296-5791
e-mail: info@mepc.org • website: www.mepc.org

MEPC was founded in 1981 to expand public discussion and understanding of current issues affecting U.S. policies in the Middle East. The council is a non-profit educational organization that offers workshops for secondary-level educators on how to teach students about the Arab world and Islam. It publishes the quarterly journal *Middle East Policy* as well as special reports and books.

Middle East Research and Information Project (MERIP)
1500 Massachusetts Ave. NW, Suite 119, Washington, DC 20005
(202) 223-3677 • fax: (202) 223-3604
website: www.merip.org

MERIP's mission is to educate the public about the contemporary Middle East, with particular emphasis on U.S. policy, human rights, and social justice issues. It publishes the quarterly magazine *Middle East Report*.

Middle East Studies Association (MESA)
1219 N. Santa Rita Ave., University of Arizona, Tucson, AZ 85721
(520) 621-5850 • fax: (520) 626-9095
e-mail: mesanau.arizona.edu • website: http://fp.arizona.edu/mesassoc

MESA is a professional academic association of scholars who specialize in the study of the Middle East, North Africa, and the Islamic world. The association runs a project for the evaluation of textbooks for coverage of the Middle East. It publishes the quarterly *International Journal of Middle East Studies*, the biannual *MESA Bulletin*, and the quarterly *MESA Newsletter*.

Washington Institute for Near East Policy
1828 L St. NW, Suite 1050, Washington, DC 20036
(202) 452-0650 • fax: (202) 223-5364
e-mail: info@washingtoninstitute.org • website: www.washingtoninstitute.org

The institute is an independent organization that produces research and analysis on the Middle East and on U.S. policy in the region. It publishes numerous books, periodic monographs, and reports on regional politics, security, and economics. Its publications include *PeaceWatch*, which focuses on the Arab-Israeli peace process, and the reports "Israeli Preconditions for Palestinian Statehood," "Democracy and Arab Political Culture," and "Democracy in the Middle East: Defining the Challenge."

BIBLIOGRAPHY

Books

Riah Abu El-Assal	*Caught in Between: The Story of an Arab Palestinian Christian Israeli.* London: SPCK, 1999.
Mitchell G. Bard	*The Complete Idiot's Guide to Middle East Conflict.* Indianapolis, IN: Alpha Books, 2003.
Eytan Bentsur	*Making Peace: A First-Hand Account of the Arab-Israeli Peace Process.* Westport, CT: Praeger, 2001.
Ahron Bregman and Jihan El-Tahri	*The Fifty Years' War: Israel and the Arabs.* New York: TV Books, 1999.
Noam Chomsky	*Fateful Triangle: The United States, Israel, and the Palestinians.* Cambridge, MA: South End Press, 1999.
Dilip Hiro	*Sharing the Promised Land: A Tale of the Israelis and Palestinians.* New York: Olive Branch Press, 1999.
Efraim Karsh, ed.	*Israel: The First Hundred Years.* Portland, OR: Frank Cass, 2000.
Haig Khatchadourian	*The Quest for Peace Between Israel and the Palestinians.* New York: Peter Lang, 2000.
Philip Mattar, ed.	*Encyclopedia of the Palestinians.* New York: Facts On File, 2000.
Benny Morris	*Righteous Victims: A History of the Zionist-Arab Conflict, 1881–1999.* New York: Knopf, 1999.
Benjamin Netanyahu	*A Durable Peace: Israel and Its Place Among the Nations.* New York: Warner Books, 2000.
Ritchie Ovendale	*The Origins of the Arab-Israeli Wars.* New York: Addison Wesley Longman, 1999.
Itamar Rabinovich	*Waging Peace: Israel and the Arabs at the End of the Century.* New York: Farrar, Straus, and Giroux, 1999.
Amnon Rubinstein	*From Herzl to Rabin: The Changing Image of Zionism.* New York: Holmes & Meier, 2000.
Edward W. Said	*The End of the Peace Process: Oslo and After.* New York: Pantheon Books, 2000.
David K. Shipler	*Arab and Jew: Wounded Spirits in a Promised Land.* New York: Penguin Books, 2002.
Avi Shlaim	*The Iron Wall: Israel and the Arab World.* New York: W.W. Norton, 2000.
Bernard Wasserstein	*Divided Jerusalem: The Struggle for the Holy City.* New Haven, CT: Yale University Press, 2002.

Periodicals

David Apgar	"A 'Virtual' Mideast Peace," *International Economy*, January 2001.
Bernard Avishai	"Tribal Warfare," *American Prospect*, August 13, 2001.

153

Mubarak E. Awad   "The Road to Arab-Israeli Peace," *Tikkun*, January
and Abdul Aziz Said   2001.

Azmi Bishara   "Arab Citizens of Palestine: Little to Celebrate,"
                         Tikkun, July/August 1998.

Roane Carey   "Letter from Palestine," *Nation*, July 23, 2001.

Christopher Dickey   "How Will Israel Survive?" *Newsweek*, April 1, 2002.
and Daniel Klaidman

Nada Elia   "Open Letter to My Anti-Racist Friends," *Off Our
                         Backs*, August/September 2002.

Jeff Halper   "Israel's War on Palestinians," *Tikkun*, May/June 1998.

Joshua Hammer   "A Shark Hunt in the Night," *Newsweek*, July 15, 2002.

Joshua Hammer   "The Way They Live Now," *Newsweek*, April 1, 2002.

Victor Davis Hanson   "History Isn't on Palestinians' Side," *Wall Street
                         Journal*, April 2, 2002.

Michael Hirsh   "Blowing the Best Chance," *Newsweek*, April 1, 2002.

Carmela Ingwer   "Risks and Faith," *Cross Currents*, Spring 1999.
                         Available from 475 Riverside Dr., New York, NY
                         10115.

Rashid I. Khalidi   "Toward a Clear Palestinian Strategy," *Journal of
                         Palestine Studies*, Summer 2002.

Maclean's   "A Fractured Dream," April 27, 1998.

Rachelle Marshall   "Israel 'Fights Terrorism' with War on the Palestinian
                         Authority," *Washington Report on Middle East Affairs*,
                         October 2001. Available from American Educational
                         Trust, Inc., PO Box 53062, Washington, DC 20009.

J.F.O. McAllister   "Two Families Under the Gun," *Time*, April 1, 2002.

Michael B. Oren   "Does the U.S. Finally Understand Israel?"
                         Commentary, July/August 2002.

Eetta Prince-Gibson   "An Israeli Dove Mourns," *Progressive*, December 2000.

Danny Rubinstein   "Israel at Fifty," *Nation*, May 4, 1998.

Elizabeth Sanders and   "After the Assault," *Christian Century*, May 8, 2002.
Marthame Sanders

Jerome Slater   "Israel, Anti-Semitism, and the Palestinian Problem,"
                         Tikkun, May 2001.

David C. Unger   "Maps of War, Maps of Peace," *World Policy Journal*,
                         Summer 2002.

Martin Van Creveld   "Build a Wall to the Sky . . ." *Newsweek*, April 1, 2001.

Mortimer B.   "Awaiting a Miracle," *U.S. News & World Report*,
Zuckerman   July 2, 2001.

Mortimer B.   "Israel's Righteous Fight," *U.S. News & World Report*,
Zuckerman   April 15, 2002.

INDEX

Abdullah (king of Jordan), 81, 137
Abraham, 13–14
Abu Eid family, 89, 90–92
Adwan, Qais, 87–88
Allenby, Edmund Henry Hynman, 18
Allon Plan (1967), 37
American Jews, 121–22, 123
Amir, Yigal, 74
Annan, Kofi, 56, 69
anti-Semitism, 132
Aqaba, Gulf of, 29
al-Aqsa intifada, 11
al-Aqsa Mosque. *See* Temple Mount
Arab-Israeli conflict
  Arabs vs. Israelis as starting, 22–23
  as bad for entire world, 132–33
  key controversies surrounding, 7–8
  roots of, 13–14, 21–22, 25
  see also Israel; Palestinians; peace
    process; violence
Arab-Israeli War (1948), 27
Arab nationalism, 57, 131
Arabs
  biblical background on, 13–14
  British promising statehood to, 26
  claims over Palestine, 25
  early attitude toward Jewish
    immigration by, 19–20
  hatred between Jews and, 131–32
  Israeli killed in auto accident by,
    100, 104
  on partition of Palestine, 27
  personal reactions to tensions and
    violence, 82–83, 85–88
  response to Israeli independence,
    23
  response to Jewish immigration to
    Palestine, 19–20, 26
  roots of suicide murder in culture
    of, 54
  as starting the Arab-Israeli conflict,
    22–23
  violence against, 101–102
  Yom Kippur War and, 30
  see also Palestinians
Arafat, Yasser
  attention paid to Palestinian cause
    by, 107–108
  Camp David negotiations and, 10,
    46, 50

  as encouraging terrorism, 10
  international allies of, 56–57
  Netanyahu and, 41
  Oslo Peace Accords and, 34, 36, 50
  peace process dilemma of, 39–40
  the PLO and, 29
  as representing the history of
    Palestinian struggles, 49
  September 2000 talks with Barak
    and, 44–45
  tactics of terror by, 55–56
  type of leadership by, 51
  as working for Israel, 39
Armstrong, Karen, 14, 15

Baker, James, 33
Balfour Declaration, 18–19, 26
Barak, Ehud, 34
  Camp David negotiations and, 10,
    46, 125, 137
  September 2000 talks with Arafat
    and, 44–45
Begin, Menachem, 19, 31
Beitler, Ruth Margolies, 25
Ben-Gurion, David, 7, 27
Bethlehem, 23
Bevenisti, Meron, 38
biblical times, 13–14, 21–22
Birnbaum, Nathan, 15
Brown, Cherie R., 114
Brownfeld, Allan C., 73, 119
Bush, George H.W., 33
Bush, George W., 45
Butler, Linda, 58

Camp David negotiations (2000), 10,
  31, 45–47, 137
Camp David II, 128
Cheney, Dick, 136
Christians
  anti-Jewish discrimination by, 14
  on Jerusalem, 23–24
  religious fundamentalism of, 73
  religious tolerance and, 15–16
Churchill, Winston, 19
Church of the Holy Sepulcher, 24
Cleveland, William L., 15
Clinton, Bill, 10, 46–47
Clinton, Chelsea, 46
Cohen, Steven M., 121

Crusades, the, 14

Dagan, Rachel, 94
Darwin, Charles, 14
David, 23
Declaration of Principles on Interim
  Self-Government Arrangements
  (DOP), 35
Diaspora, 22
Diaspora nationalism, 131
Dome of the Rock, 24
Donnelly, John, 106
Dreyfus, Alfred, 15

East Jerusalem, 24
Egypt, 16
  Israeli attack on, 29
  PLO and, 29
  return of Sinai desert by, 31
  Suez Canal and, 28
  taking Gaza Strip, 27–28
Eisen, Arnold M., 121
England, 128–29
Erakat, Saeb, 85–86
Europe, 56–57, 134

Facts and Logic About the Middle
  East (FLAME), 65
families
  mourning by, 87, 89–93
  stories by mothers, 94–98
Fatah, 29
Fields-Meyer, Thomas, 89
Firestone, Reuven, 76–77
France, 18, 19
  anti-Semitism in, 57
  the Suez Canal and, 28
Franji, Abdullah, 98

Gaza Strip
  Egypt taking, 27–28
  Israeli occupation of, as issue in
    peace process, 9
  Israel's acquisition of, 8, 29
  in Oslo Peace Accords, 35, 39
  Palestinian uprising in, 30–32
  Rabin's goal for, 37–38
Germany, 123
Golan Heights
  Israel's acquisition of, 8, 29
  Syria taking control over, 28
Goldberg, J.J., 21
Goldstein, Baruch, 74
Goodman, Elliot, 75
Great Britain

Balfour Declaration and, 18–19, 26
capturing lands in the Middle East,
  17–18, 22
Jordan and, 22
limiting Jewish immigration, 19
promise to Arabs on their
  independence, 26
the Suez Canal and, 28
Greniman, Deborah French, 99
Gulf War, 33

Hamas
  Arafat and, 39
  personal account from member of,
    87–88
  Rabin's deportation of, 34
  suicide attacks and, 41, 60–61
Har Homa, 40
Hebron, 23
Hebron agreement (1997), 10
Herzl, Theodor, 15, 53–54
Hess, Moses, 14–15
Holocaust, the, 22, 115
Holy Land Foundation, 60–61
Husay-McMahon agreement, 26
Hussain (sharif of Mecca), 18

IDF (Israeli Defense Forces), 66
immigration
  to Israel, 123
  Jewish, to Palestine, 16–17, 19–20,
    25–26
  aggressive recruitment of,
    120–21, 123–24
  Arab attitudes toward, 19–20
intifada, 30–32
  comparison of first and second,
    58–59
  Israeli law and, 65–66
Iraq, 26
Irgun (terrorist organization), 19
Isaac, 13–14
Islam, suicide killings and, 61
Israel
  attack on Egypt, 28, 29
  attention paid to Palestinian cause
    by, 107–108
  birth of, 7, 27, 108
  factors leading to intifada and,
    31–32
  50th birthday celebration of, 107,
    108
  impact of Six-Day War on, 29–30
  Jerusalem and, 24
  as the Jewish "homeland," 119–20

Jewish immigration to, 16–17, 19–20, 25–26
Jewish settlements in, 31–32, 33
Jewish vs. Arab claims to, 21–22
Jews can be at home without living in, 122–23
must accept a Palestinian state, 70–71
as needing a European support system, 134
occupation of Israeli territories, 8–10, 23
in Oslo II, 38
precariousness of position of, 138–39
refusal to acknowledge religious extremism in, 75
as a society based on law, 65–67
media coverage of, 68–69
on refugee camps, 69
see also violence, Israeli
Israelis
conflicting points of view among, 100, 103
as fighting for space, 104–105
funeral of, 100–101
killed in auto accident by Arabs, 100, 104
reacting to loss of a daughter, 89, 92–93
on refugee issue, 8
rights gained through Oslo Peace Accords, 35, 36–37, 38–39
routine morning of, 99
stories reacting to violence from, 94–95, 97
traveling on dangerous roads, 102–103
violence against, 126–27
see also Jews
Israeli War of Independence, 7

Jabotinsky, Vladimir, 40
Jerusalem
British taking over, 17–18
as a crucial issue, 30
division of, 133
expansion of Jewish settlements in, 40
as an idea vs. an address, 122
importance of, 23–24
Israelis gaining control of, 30
see also Temple Mount
Jewish Defense League (JDL), 74
Jewish nationalism, 130–31

Jewish settlements, 31–32
expansion of, 40–41
as preventing peace, 133
removal of, 134
violence in, 41
Jews
as being at home around the world, 122–23
biblical background on, 13–14
claims over Palestine, 25
claims to Israel by, 21–22
as growing population in Israel, 121
hatred between Arabs and, 131–32
have given up too much land, 127–28
immigration to Palestine by, 14, 16–17, 19–20, 25–26
Israel as "homeland" to, 119–20
Israel as a peripheral interest for American, 121–22
on Jerusalem, 23–24
living in occupied territories, 9–10
obstacles to participation in peace process by, 114–16
personal reactions to tensions and violence by, 80–82, 83–85
pogroms of, 14
religious fundamentalism among, 73–75
religious tolerance and, 15–16
Russian, 123
suggestion of a "national home" in Palestine for, 14–15
Zionism's goals for, 53–54
John Paul II (pope), 54–55
Jordan, 22, 27–28
Jospin, Lionel, 57

Katsev, Moshe, 120
Kilani, Zakariya, 88
Kissinger, Henry A., 136
Klausner, C.L., 15

land for peace policy, 125, 127, 128–29
Latner, Craig, 75
Lawrence , Thomas Edward (T.E.), 18
Lebanon, 51
Leci, Colin, 125
Levinger, Moshe, 75
Levy, David, 40
Likud party, 19, 31–32
Limor family, 89, 92–93
Lloyd George, David, 19

Madrid Conferences, 33–34
Malley, Bob, 46
Al-Masri, Ahmed Salem, 106, 108–12
McCarthy, Justin, 17
McMahon, Sir Henry, 18
Menocal, Maria Rosa, 16
Mesopotamia, 26
military. See IDF
Mitchell, George, 45
Mitchell Report, 11
mothers, mourning by, 87
Muasher, Marwan, 56
Mubarak, Hosni, 81
Muhammad, 15–16
Munich Olympics (1972), 55
Muslims
    on Jerusalem, 23–24
    religious tolerance and, 15–16

Nasser, Gamal Abdel, 28, 29
nationalism
    Arab, 131
    Jewish, 130–31
    Palestinian, 26–27
    as preventing peace, 133
Netanyahu, Benjamin, 40–41
    on Oslo Peace Accords, 40
Neturei Karta, 15

Ornament of the World, The (Menocal),
    16
Oslo Peace Accords (1993), 9, 132
    agreements in, 34–35, 50
    Palestinian critique of, 36–37
    Rabin and, 34, 37–38
    recognition letters in, 35–36
Oslo II, 38
Ottoman Empire, 16
Oz, Amos, 34–35

Palestine
    Arab population in, 19
    Arab states taking land from, 27
    British control of, 26
    early suggestion of a Jewish
        "national home" in, 14–15
    Jewish immigration to, 14, 19–20,
        25–26
    Jewish population in, 17, 19, 121
    partitioning of, 7, 71
    pre-1967 border in, 137
    UN partitioning of, 27
Palestine Liberation Organization
    (PLO)
    creation of, 29

criticism of, 39
intifada and, 32
weakening of, 34
Palestinian National Council, 10
Palestinian nationalism, 26–27, 57
Palestinians
    Barak's generous offer to, 125–26
    Camp David negotiations and,
        114–15
    core issues of current struggle by,
        45–46
    do not teach hatred, 60–61
    endurance of, 64
    factors leading to intifada by,
        30–32
    impact of Six-Day War on, 29–30
    Israeli violence against
        as destroying civilian life, 69
        media coverage of, 68–69
        is not justified, 70
    Israel must accept sovereign
        existence of, 70–71
    mothers' stories on loss, 95–98
    on Oslo Peace Accords, 36–37
    rights gained through, 35, 36,
        38–39
    in Oslo II, 38
    reacting to loss of a son, 89, 90–92
    violence by
        comparison of first and second
            intifadas in, 58–59
        as predating the state of Israel,
            54, 55
        psychological factors of, 59–60
        willingness to forgive and forget,
            58–59
peace process
    efforts at, 10–11
    eight principles of, 116–17
    an imposed settlement for, 134–35
    Israeli withdrawal from occupied
        territories and, 23
    Israel must make concessions to
        Palestine in, 71–72
    Jewish people giving up land will
        not help, 125–29
    Jewish settlements as preventing,
        133
    Jews have given up too much land
        for, 127–28
    nationalism as preventing, 133
    need for U.S. role in, 133–34,
        136–37, 139–40
    obstacles to Jewish participation in,
        114–16

partition of Palestine by, 27
position of Israel as a" Jewish
homeland" is an obstacle to,
119–20
precariousness of Israeli position
in, 138–39
proposal for, by Crown Prince
Abdullah, 137–38
refugee issue and, 8, 28
restoring hope in, 118
September 2000 talks and, 44–45
setback in, 49–50
Taba, Egypt, talks and, 47
violence and, 43–44
see also Camp David negotiations;
Madrid Conferences; Oslo Peace
Accords
People of the Book, 16
Peres, Shimon, 40–41
Peretz, Martin, 53
Pinsker, Leo, 15
pogroms, 14

Qawasmeh, Fathiyeh, 95

Rabin, Yitzhak
assassination of, 40, 73–75, 77
Jewish settlements increased under,
40–41
on Jewish territories, 34
Oslo Peace Accords and, 34, 36,
37–38, 50
Rees, Matt, 94
refugees/refugee camps, 23
fleeing their homes, 109–10
Israeli violence and, 69
as issue in peace negotiations, 8
life of Palestinian, 108–109
peace process and, 28
personal account from schoolgirl
in, 86–87
as remaining, 108
returning to their homes, 110–12
visit to native village by,
106–107
Regev, Uri, 75–76
religious fundamentalism
in Christianity, 73
fighting, 77–78
increase in Israeli, 75–76
in Judaism, 73–75
refusal to acknowledge, 75
religious tolerance, 15–16
roads, dangerous, 102–103
Rothschild, Edmond de, 17

Rothschild, Lord Lionel Walter, 18

Sadat, Anwar, 31
Said, Edward, 34–35, 36, 68
San Remo Peace Conference (1920),
26
Sarah, 13–14
El Sarraj, Eyad, 58
al-Sayfi, Kiyan Khaled, 86–87
Schafer, David, 13
Schmemann, Serge, 40, 49, 69
Seidman, Dorit, 97
September 11 terrorist attacks, 73,
75–76, 132–33
Shaath, Nabil, 35
al-Shafi, 'Abd, 35
Shamas, Maha, 96
Shamir, Yitzhak, 33
Sharon, Ariel
Camp David negotiations and, 50
cycle of violence and, 51–52
on Israeli right to land, 70
on pogroms, 14
as representing the history of
Israeli struggles, 49
type of leadership by, 50–51
see also Temple Mount
Shlomot, Moria, 82
Sinai Desert, 8, 29
Six-Day War, 23, 29–30
Soviet Union, 123
Sudo, Phil, 21
Suez Canal, 16, 28
Suez Crisis of 1956, 28
suicide attacks
Arab/Muslim roots of, 54
celebration of, 62
debate on damage from, 62–63
debated among Muslims, 61
following Sharon's visit to Temple
Mount, 11
in Jerusalem, 41
Hamas and, 60
PLO terror tactics and, 55–56
psychological reasons for, 59–60
Sykes-Picot Agreement (1916), 18, 19
Syrians, 28

Taba, Egypt, talks (2001), 38, 47
Tawil, Sheik Jamal, 82–83
Temple Mount
Sharon's visit to, 10–11, 45, 50
tensions following, 80–88
terrorist acts. See violence
Thomas, Baylis, 33

Tibon, Noam, 84–85
Time (magazine), 80
Transjordan, 22
Triestman, Atara, 80–81
Tye, Larry, 122, 123
Tzameret, Nitza, 97–98

United Nations
  General Assembly Resolution 194,
    8, 108
  Israel supported by, 7
  partition of Palestine by, 27
  Security Council Resolution 181, 7
  Security Council Resolution 242, 8,
    23, 30
United States
  attitude of American Jews in,
    121–22
  Camp David negotiations and, 44,
    45, 46
  number of Israeli Jews in, 123
  role of, in peace process, 133–34,
    136–37, 139–40
Urban II (pope), 14

Vilbig, Peter, 43
violence
  against Arabs, 101–102
  Arafat's tactics of terror, 55–56
  comparison of first and second
    intifadas, 58–59
  continues Middle East conflict,
    41–42
  cycle of, 49–52, 89–90, 132–33
  debate on justification for
    Palestinian, 10
  examples of, 43
  families responding to losses from,
    90–93
  Israeli
    as destroying Palestinian civil
      life, 69
    is not justified, 70
    Jewish Holy War and, 76–77
    media coverage of, 68–69
    on refugee camps, 69

  restraint from, 66–67
  against Israelis, 126–27
  John Paul II and, 54–55
  long term effects of, 63
  mothers' stories on, 94–98
  Palestinian Intifada (1987), 30–32
  personal stories on tensions from,
    80–88
  as predating the state of Israel, 54,
    55
  psychological factors of, 59–60
  religious fundamentalism and,
    73–78
  during Sharon's visit to Temple
    Mount, 50
  see also suicide attacks

Weizman, Ezer, 120
Weizmann, Chaim, 18–19
West Bank
  Israeli occupation of, as issue in
    peace process, 9–10
  Israel's acquisition of, 8, 29
  Jordan taking, 27–28
  in Oslo Peace Accords, 35, 39
  in Oslo II, 38
  Palestinians' current issue on,
    45–46
  Palestinian uprising in, 30–32
  the PLO and, 32
Western Wall, the, 23
"White Papers," 19
Wine, Sherwin, 130
Women's Center for Legal Aid and
  Counseling, 96
Wye Memorandum, 10

Yatom, Danny, 81–82, 83–84
Yom Kippur War (1973), 30

Zionism, 22, 123–24
  Arab hatred of, 131
  birth of, 14–15
  goals of, 53–54
  resistance to, 15
Zionist nationalism, 131